Celebrating Poetry

2014 Poetry Anthology

Karenzo Media

Celebrating Poetry: 2014 Poetry Anthology

Edited by Karen Hamilton Silvestri

Karenzo Media
North Carolina, USA
Queensland, Australia
www.karenzomedia.com

NOTE: Some authors use British English, some use American English. Other than light editing for structure and typos, I have not altered the spellings of words in these narratives. – *Karen Hamilton Silvestri*

CONTRIBUTING AUTHORS:

Merlene Fawdry, Tanya Fernbank, Andrew Goggans, Kathleen Kline, Nicholas McKay, Bob McNeil, Mairi Neil, Trinity Renee, Timothy Rodriguez, Ailene Rogers, Susan Skvorc, Enzo Silvestri, Karen Silvestri, Samantha Stemler, Sarah Taylor

COVER ART AND DESIGN: Karen Hamilton Silvestri

LAYOUT: Karen Hamilton Silvestri, www.karenzomedia.net

ISBN **978-0-9899318-7-8**

The Poet's Idea Notebook

Poet's record emotion more than anything else. What cannot be expressed by the telling, the poet seeks to tell by using everyday objects, places, and people to get across an emotion. It is highly recommended that you keep a notebook of some sort that you can jot down ideas as they come to you.

Think of your notebook as your portable filing cabinet. **Good writers throw NOTHING away**. You may never use what you put in your Idea Notebook, but the act of keeping ideas will help to generate more ideas! Get in the habit of carrying it with you always, as you never know when you'll want to jot something down before it's forgotten.

This workbook contains blank ruled pages where you can try out the exercises or make notes as you read the exercises. Don't be afraid to write in your workbook! Many of these exercises come straight from my own poet's notebooks that I have kept over the years!

Suggested ideas for your notebook

People Watching - observations about the people around you

Eavesdropping - re-creations of conversations you hear

Descriptions - descriptions of the world around you

Words - New words you encounter

Reflections - thoughts and feelings regarding your day

Poetry - other peoples or your own

Dreams (Yours or your buddy's! No one is safe from an artist!)

Found stuff - lines from novels or movies

First Lines and titles - first lines or titles for poems, stories, or other pieces

Quotes - cool quotes you hear or read

By concentrating on the sounds, on the quality of the verbal music, and the strangeness of the juxtapositions rather than on the "meaning," one often comes closer to the secret language of the unconscious." – Steven Kowit

In the Palm of Your Hand: the Poet's Portable Workshop. Maine: Tilbury House, 1995.

Nuts and Bolts

Line and Stanza Breaks:
- Drop one line to indicate a comma
- Drop a stanza to indicate period
- Hear where your line breaks
- When writing poetry as narrative, a line break should create a pause in your story. Think of this pause as a transition from variations of emotions. You may move from peace to uncertainty to anger to peace again.

Repetition and Rhyme
- Repetition is the 20th century version of rhyme

Tense
- Present tense is always more effective in poetry

Cutting words
- Get rid of every 'to be' verb and 'have/have not' type verbs
- Get rid of prepositions, articles, etc. They don't do any work for your poem!

Poetic Devices

Poetic Device	Definition
Simile	a comparison using "as" or "like"
Alliteration	the deliberate repetition of consonant sounds
Metaphor	a comparison not using as or like when one thing is said to be another
Rhyme	repetition of same sounds
Rhythm	internal 'feel' of beat and metre perceived when poetry is read aloud
Onomatopoeia	"sound echoing sense"; use of words resembling the sounds they mean
Oxymoron	a seeming contradiction in two words put together
Rhyming Couplet	a pair of lines which end-rhyme expressing one clear thought
Personification	attribution of human motives or behaviours to impersonal agencies
Hyperbole	exaggeration for dramatic effect

Essays about Poetry

Understanding *Free verse* and *Blank Verse Poetry Forms*

Merlene Fawdry

Blank Verse and Free Verse are probably the most misunderstood and misused forms of poetry. With many people viewing both as not being 'real' poetry, and others believing the throwing down of random words on paper or computer screen is Free Verse, it is important to understand the qualities of each before either can be used correctly.

Free Verse, also called open form verse, comes from the French 'vers libre'. Unlike traditional verse, its rhythms are not organized into the regularity of meter and most often lack rhyme. This differs from Blank Verse, which has as its form unrhymed iambic pentameter. It is worth mentioning here the confusion that often arises between Free Verse and prose and how one distinguishes between the two. Without the structure or rules that apply to traditional poetry, sometimes poets new to the art simply write prose in poetic form. This is not Free Verse. Unlike prose, which is arranged in sentence and paragraph form, Free Verse has a deliberate division of the lines. These may consist of a string of words or a single word and may be divided mid-sentence or even mid-word to create the desired effect.

Blank Verse, although appearing easy to write, requires greater creativity and depth of thought than many other verse forms if it is to meet the demands of the necessary variety. Its unrhymed lines of iambic pentameter consist of ten syllables, with the second, fourth, sixth, eighth, and tenth syllables accented. This is the form generally accepted for dramatic verse in English and commonly used for long poems whether dramatic, philosophical, or narrative.

While Free Verse poetry does not adhere to the conventional use of meter, it is based on the recurrence of irregular rhythmic cadence and has variations of phrases, images and syntactical patterns and many poetic language and devices. When rhyme is used, it does not follow any distinct rhyme scheme or pattern, but shapes the poem around the poet's thoughts and ideas. Ideas and expression of thought are linked through the use of alliteration, assonance and imagery.

Therefore the difference between Blank verse and Free Verse can be seen to be structural. Both may be unrhymed, but Free Verse is basically irregular verse that flows without following any particular metrical pattern while

Blank Verse follows a metrical pattern, which is usually iambic pentameter.

Rhyme and Meter in Poetry
Merlene Fawdry

Rhyme and meter are used in poetry to reflect the tone or subject matter by complimenting the word choices the poet makes in its creation.

Rhyming is a poetic device defined as the repetition of two similar sounds in two or more different words. It enhances the rhythm or cadence of the poem by adding another dimension. Rhyming can add amusement and interest to a poem if done well; however, when used gratuitously it is cumbersome and lacks spontaneity.

Many novice poets view the rhyming or coupling with similar sounding words as all that is needed to create poetry, often taking a concept that has creative merit and reducing its quality through forced end rhyme. Others appear to have difficulty discerning the difference between a well written rhyming poem and doggerel – a nonsense poem better suited to comedy and satire or children's rhyming games.

While experimenting with lines and phrases and poetic devices is always desirable in creating a poem in a fresh, extraordinary way, one that is pleasing to the eye and ear, the forcing of rhyme, in which the natural order of words is reversed to manipulate language for rhyming conformity detracts from the natural flow a poem should have. When rhyme is the primary focus, it will detract from the tone and subject and the overall value of the poem.

Sometimes, this issue may not be as much about the forcing of rhyme as against the adherence to a rhyming pattern that is simply not working. In this instance it is better to look at alternative rhyming patterns and choose one better suited to that particular work.

Meter is the pattern of stressed and unstressed syllables in a line of poetry. Each meter is comprised of units called feet and a foot is a unit of rhythm within the meter. Different traditions and genres of poetry tend to use different meters. Shakespeare showed a preference for iambic pentameter, Homer wrote in dactylic hexameter, while nursery rhymes are often written in anapaestic tetrameter.

Variations to established meter are common and used to avoid uninteresting repetition and provide emphasis or attention where the poem requires it. This may involve inverting the stress in a foot or adding a pause, known as a caesura, in place of this. Some metric patterns, such as iambic pentameter (ten syllable lines of five iambs) tend to be regular, while others vary between languages where different distinct patterns often develop.

So, while rhyme is useful and an often desirable poetic device, it needs to be used in conjunction with other devices to heighten language and sound. It is also important for the poet to determine the tone they are seeking for their subject and choose their words to accommodate this, rather than making the poem accommodate a single, or series of, rhyming words.

What is Post-Modern American Poetry?

Karen Hamilton Silvestri

Following World War II, with the bombing of Japan, the cohesive center disappeared for Americans. People began to move outward from the cities and into newly created suburbs. Women did not wish to return to the world of housekeeping after tasting the freedom of war-time employment. Minorities also felt the impact of a newly found freedom. We split the atom, the center of everything, and in so doing we created chaos. The Contemporary Poets reflect this chaos.

The characteristics of Post-Modern Poetry include many modernist themes and many modernist themes taken to new levels. The largest indicator of Post-modern poetry is the "absence of a single dominant style" (Norton 2649). Other characteristics include, "Mix of image with narrative, mix of image with discursive, precise observation, philosophical reflection, open-ended juxtaposition, multiple stories, alterations in Point of View, digressions, no coherence or closure, and unexpected jumps & disjunctive thinking" (Norton 2647). There is also "an apprehension of the invisible world, fragmentation" (Norton 2646), and a style that appears to be a "poetic diary or journal" (Norton 2646).

The contemporary poets see language as a means of reaching the inner self and the emotion that is difficult to give voice to. The twentieth century ushered in many new discoveries, most importantly the discovery of psychoanalysis by Sigmund Freud. The advent of psychoanalysis gave people the means of accessing the individuals' inner self. Modern poets sought to explore the inner workings of the individual as a human being, giving a concrete language to emotion.

One of the most recognized poets of this time, T.S. Eliot, brought to the world of poetry an aesthetic form that was full of complex twists and turns, fragmented language, and a sense of alienation and loss. The Modern poets viewed their art as more than a venue to affect change in society and the individual, they began to focus on language itself and how it relates to the individuals perception of the world. As the world rapidly changed around them, poets like Eliot sought to capture the sense of chaos and fragmentation with the written word.

In his most famous poem, *"The Wasteland"*, Eliot manages to lament (and celebrate) the chaos of modern culture. The poem is chaotic and fragmented, embodying the very nature of modern society. As the world careened out of control around the individual with the advent of World War, fractured societies, and multiple religions, Eliot's poem whirls through time and space, capturing the insanity and loss in the very language he uses. "The Wasteland" encompasses a myriad of characters undergoing extreme stress and anxiety, "Speak to me. /who do you never speak. Speak. What are you thinking of? What thinking? What? I never know what you are thinking. Think" (Eliot 495). These characters personify the complex ideologies of the time period.

Different poets used similar ways of conveying emotion into language. Paul Celen calls his poetry, the "poem, the noem" In German this means "gedicht, das genicht", which translates to 'poem, not poem'; in other words, "poem negated" (Mitchell). Language can name the pain but it can't be the pain, language cannot reach the actual individual feeling. How do you articulate the nothing? Something is there and then suddenly it is gone. Language is not strong enough to convey the intense emotion. What needs to be conveyed is so horrific and deep that it is difficult for the average person to comprehend or if they can comprehend it they draw back from the intensity of it. The contemporary poets seek to use language to reach that intense emotion.

Wallace Stevens believed that the reality you are experiencing is your emotional state at any given time. We respond to our interpretations of what happens, not what has happened. This gives you an emotional state, an emotional state that reinforces and affects interpretation that in turn affects emotions. As we translate the material world into words we change the material world (Mitchell).

Gwendolyn Brooks uses irregular lines and sudden rhythm to convey the emotion of anger and indifference. Her voice is one of passionate observation that expresses love and rage. In "a song in the front yard", Brooks explores the class distinctions of the ghettos. The poem illuminates the human condition of presenting polished aspects of our personality to the masses while harboring a wild, untamed personality on the inside. Note that the front yard is tended carefully, while the back yard is left wild. "I ant a peek at the back Where it's rough and untended and hungry weed grows. A girl gets sick of a rose" (Brooks 2780). The outside nurtures something wild within. Creating a dyad, Brooks makes what is unfamiliar inside, what is familiar is outside.

It is interesting to note that Modern Poetry laments loss and fragmentation, while Post-Modern Poetry celebrates it. There are notions of whole fragments that don't link to any conclusion. Anne Lauderbach suggests that as our lives are made up of strings of fragments, so is post-modern poetry. Coherence is the falsehood. If we insist on neatness we will leave out something of significance - too neat is false, you experience nothing. Fragments create variety (Lauderbach).

In interpreting Modern Poetry it is not necessary to understand the poets exact meaning. It is sufficient that the reader take from a poem what they need to take, which may not be what the writer intended. But that is okay because the reader takes the feeling; they get in touch with the emotion. To paraphrase John Ashbery, "You, the reader, add the flowers to the field with your interpretation" (Mitchell). The poet creates an openness, an empty field and the reader connects with the emotion and fills the field with fragments, creating a whole. The Modern Poets are teaching us to see the world in different ways than we are used to. Readers have to learn to dance to the new music.

Finally, modern poetry creates a mythology of human psyche and culture by delving into how language works, as well as exploring subject and content. A poem is not a puzzle to be solved but an experience, an event to take part in. The modern poets created metapoems, which are poems about how poems and language operate. They have no fixed center; it is "a hymn to possibility" as John Ashbery says. The modern poet, Anne Lauderbach says, "Depart from the tune - breaking the form is the form. We explore the world through forms" (Lauderbach). By breaking traditional form and exploring the complexities of language itself, the contemporary poet embarks on an adventure of self-discovery, forging new roads into the inner workings of individuals and their societies.

Works Cited

1.   Brooks, Gwendolyn. "a song in the front yard." Norton Anthology of American Literature. Sixth Edition, Vol. E. Ed. Nina Baym. New York: W.W. Norton & Company, 2003. 2780-2781.

2.   Eliot, T.S. "The Wasteland." Norton Anthology of Modern Poetry. 2nd Edition, Ed. Ellmann, Richard and O'Clair, Robert. New York: W.W. Norton & Company, 1998. 491-504.

3.   Lauderbach, Anne. Notes from Lauderbach's lecture at Florida Atlantic University, Boca Raton, Florida, 1/30/01

4.   Mitchell, Susan. 2001. LIT 3021 Modern Poetry. Florida Atlantic University, Boca Raton, Florida.

The Exact Word: Analyzing Word Choice in Two Poems by Emily Dickinson

Karen Hamilton Silvestri

"I dwell in Possibility" (No. 657)
"The Soul selects her own Society" (No. 303)

Biographer Henry Wells says of Emily Dickinson in Introduction to Emily Dickinson, "She clearly thought even more diligently of the individual words than of any other feature of a poem" (Wells 276). According to Wells, Emily lived for her poetry. Every word of her poetry is carefully chosen; each image carefully constructed using the exact word. In two of her poems, "I dwell in Possibility" (No. 657) and "The Soul selects her own Society" (No. 303) Dickinson shows her diligence to the word and she creates a theme of authority with her word choices in each of the poems.

In "The Soul selects her own Society", Dickinson seeks to invoke an image of authority through the careful choosing of the precise word. In this poem she uses words such as "divine", "Chariots", "Emperor", and "nation" to call forth the image of authority. Perhaps the poet sees herself as better than the "Majority". She is "unmoved" by the attention that they lavish on her because she perceives herself better than the "vast Majority".

In this interpretation the imagery suggested by this lofty tone is pointedly superior. She has "an Emperor kneeling Upon her Mat" - her mat. The idea of a regal Emperor - and you may picture the Emperor in his flowing, ornate robes - actually kneeling before a common woman - is an image that sets the tone of superiority. The reader can 'see' the "ample nation" begging for her attention and 'see' her point at one then turn away from the rest. "Like Stone" is a concrete image of the poet herself shutting out all that she does not desire.

Yet another analysis' of the images in "The Soul selects her own Society" are that they create a theme analogous to God and the universe. The "Soul" as the human being sees herself as god-like, she creates a universe of her own choosing by creating a defined space with her carefully chosen words - "Door", "Gate" - which keep the external world out. Whereas God has created 'Heaven' for His personal space, the poet's haven is not grand, but simple - "low Gate", "her Mat". The poet is the 'common man' who becomes superior through linguistic word play. The suggestion of superiority as stated above infer that the soul has given herself 'heavenly' qualities.

Each word has been carefully chosen by Dickinson to convey her message.

The search for the exact word is the actual theme in Dickinson's poem "I dwell in Possibility". In this poem she speculates on the craft of poetry. The poet loves words and delights in the vast number of words that she has to choose from. She sees poetry as having infinite "Possibility", whereas prose is more limiting. There are more "Windows" in poetry, more opportunities to portray the imagination.

Through poetry, the poet is free to make nouns verbs, adjectives nouns, verbs adjectives. For example, "I dwell in Possibility" - should this be read as a noun, as a place? One word has many meanings and Emily concentrated on searching for the 'exact' word. Wells remarks on Emily's word choices, "Each principal word in a major lyric constitutes for her the equivalent of a universe" (Wells 279).

Alternatively, another reading of this poem suggests that the windows symbolize the vast expanse of the universe, of the imagination, while the solid doors symbolize a limited space, thus the windows of the imagination are "More numerous" and "Superior" to "Doors—Of Chambers as the Cedars". The poet "dwells" in the imagination, in deep thought and contemplation, a place she finds more comforting than the vast exterior world she calls "Prose". The imagination dwells in the soul's self, "Impregnable of Eye" it is accessible only to the creator.

Further, the fairest visitors could also be the words themselves. Given Emily's penchant for choosing the exact word, this is the reading that I would give the lines, "Of Visitors—the fairest—For Occupation". The fairest visitors could also refer to the people that are allowed access to the poet's world, those allowed to read the poem, perhaps those who are able to understand the poem.

Lastly, the poet once again approaches the god-like by "spreading wide my narrow Hands To gather Paradise". She has created a poem, a work of art - she has taken from the imagination an elusive being and brought it to life in the external world. Wells says, "Each poem becomes a telegram from "infinity" (Wells 283). In an essence Dickinson has created "Paradise" - the Adam and Eve and Garden of Eden liberated through the words of the poet. She has given to the universe a piece of herself.

Works Cited
1.   Dickinson, Emily. "The Soul Selects her own Society". Lawall, Sarah. (Ed.). (2003).

The Norton Anthology of World Literature, (Second Edition, Vol. E). New York: W.W. Norton & Company

2.   Dickinson, Emily. "I dwell in Possibility". Lawall, Sarah. (Ed.). (2003). The Norton Anthology of World Literature, (Second Edition, Vol. E). New York: W.W. Norton & Company

3.   Taliercio, Kathi M. "Major Symbols and Images found in 'I dwell in Possibility'." American Literature Research and Analysis Web Site. Created December 1996. Last Updated December 1996. University of South Florida in Fort Myers. Downloaded 11/25/02. http://itech.fgcu.edu/faculty/wohlpart/alra/edi dwell.htm.

4.   Wells, Henry. (1947).   Introduction to Emily Dickinson. Chicago, Illinois: Packard and Company, Hendricks House.

The Poetics of Carol Muske and Joy Harjo

Karen Hamilton Silvestri

I began a study of autobiography and memoir writing several years ago. Recently I discovered two poets who believe that recording one's place in history is integral to their art. Carol Muske and Joy Harjo are renowned poets who explore the intricacies of self in regards to cultural and historical place. Muske specifically addresses the poetics of women poets, while Harjo addresses the poetics of minority, specifically Native American, writers. Both poets emphasize the autobiographical nature of poetry. Muske and Harjo regard the self as integral to their art. In this representation of self, Muske and Harjo discuss the importance of truth-telling testimony and history in their poetics. Muske says, "...testimony exists to confront a world beyond the self and the drama of the self, even the world of silence—or the unanswerable..." (Muske 16).

Muske asks, "The question of self, for a woman poet...is continually vexing...what is a woman's self?" (Muske 3). Women have historically had their self created for them by the patriarchal society in which they live, which leaves contemporary women wondering how to define a woman's self at all. Even if they, as women, can create a self, how accurate is it? Muske muses on what is a truth telling self since a woman's perception of truth is colored always by what the patriarchal society is telling her is truth. Muske says in her poem "A Private Matter", "…there are the words, dialogue of people you once became or not…" It is in these words that a woman finds herself, a poem of all the selves in a self, but not without a cost. In "Epith", Muske muses:

> You forget yourself
> with each glittering pin,
> each chip off the old rock,
> each sip of the long toast
> to your famous independence,
> negotiated at such cost—
> and still refusing to fit.

"The inclination to bear witness seems aligned with the missing self" (Muske 4). Women create the 'missing' self by telling their stories, not the stories that have been told to them by a male dominated society, but those stories that define that missing self. In so doing, Muske reiterates the statement James Olney makes when he says, "… even as the autobiographer fixes limits in the past, a new experiment in living, a new experience in consciousness ... and a new projection or metaphor of a new self is under way" (Olney). Muske encourages contemporary women writers to produce a text that is "a model, a shape of poetic discourse based roughly on the act of testimony" (Muske 11). Harjo notes the many selves of a self who are fighting to be heard in her poem, "She Had Some Horses":

> She had horses who screamed out of fear of the silence, who carried knives to protect themselves from ghosts.
> She had horses who waited for destruction.
> She had horses who waited for resurrection.
> She had some horses.
> Harjo breaks the silence of the "missing" self by recording each self in this poem. She continues:
> She had horses who tried to save her, who climbed in her bed at night and prayed as they raped her.
> She had some horses.
> She had some horses she loved.
> She had some horses she hated.

The missing self is aligned with the self and made whole. . The poem concludes, "They were the same horses". Harjo integrates through her poem all the selves into a whole.

Inherent in discovering the missing self is the act of testimony. Muske talks of Adrienne Rich and Sylvia Plath as women poets who have changed the face of female poetics with their own truth-telling testimonies. She quotes Rich as saying, "…testimony exists to confront a world beyond the self" (Muske 16). Telling the truth, for a woman, is a breaking of imposed silence. The world beyond the self is constantly reminding women of their 'place' and women poets need to move beyond the male gaze, they need to move outside and beyond the silence. Muske admonishes the woman poet to break the silence, to speak the forbidden.

Muske notes that even this truth-telling testimony can have its problems. "…there is in the writerly imagination a deep ungovernable impulse to invent, fictionalize, to tell the truth, but (tell it) slant" (Muske 25). There are instances when perception of the truth can color the testimony, however, the larger truth is that each perception can carry the seeds of accuracy. As the self encounters changes, so do the truths of that self. A perception of one event can be perceived quite differently at a later time. In Notes from the Underground, Fydor Dostoyevsky says that "…a true autobiography is almost an impossibility, and that man is bound to lie about himself" (Dostoyevsky).

I considered
how we twisted into ourselves to live.
When the storm stopped, I sat still,
listening.
Here were the words of the Blind Poet--
crumpled like wash for the line, to be
dried, pressed flat. Upstairs, someone
called
my name. What sense would it ever
make to them, the unread world, the
getters and spenders,
if they could not hear what I heard,
not feel what I felt
nothing ruined poetry, a voice revived it,
extremity.

"if they could not hear what I heard..." is a powerful testament to the interpretation of the self and to the poem itself. For Muske, the power of poetry lies in reviving the truth over and over again. The fact that the reader will 'hear' or not 'hear' the truth is irrelevant, it is the act of testifying that bears the power of "a new language".

For Harjo, the act of truth-telling testimony is important for a different reason. "The poet is charged with the role of being the truth teller of the culture, of the times" (Harjo 141). Harjo's poems tell the truth of the Indian Nations loss and their struggle to regain a sense of identity. For Harjo, truth-telling is a way of remembering and she believes that 'remembering' is alive and affects the future. "The sheer weight of memory coupled with imagery constructs poems" (Harjo 55), Harjo says. Her poetry certainly accomplishes this as she 'remembers' the lives of her ancestors and those who have fallen in their quest for identity. Harjo says, "…there is something about poetry that demands the truth…" (Harjo 141). Through the poetic discourse of testimony, Harjo presents the truth of her people.

Both poets feel that through this act of testimony, this breaking of silence, that a new language is emerging – a language of truth. Harjo says, "I truly feel there is a new language coming about…" (Harjo 63). By reconnecting with the past and having the courage to 'speak' the truth of that past, poets achieve a level of understanding of lost cultures – the culture of silenced women and the culture of silenced Native Americans.

Muske notes in her review of *Talking to Strangers* by Patricia Dobler that "In most assimilation stories, to succeed at being American is to fail to be one's true (traditional) self" (Muske 119). This is certainly true of the Native Americans who were forcibly assimilated. Harjo offers her people a new voice to speak with, a voice that is allowed to speak of "one's true self".

Joy Harjo deeply feels the presence of those forgotten in her poetry. Harjo feels that it is very important for writers of all genders, races, and nationalities to have an understanding of their cultural and personal histories. "Sometimes I feel like specters of forgotten ones roam the literature of some of these American writers who don't understand where they come from, who they are, where they are going..." (Harjo 70). Harjo discusses the importance of recording one's roots and remembering, both of which are central to Native Americans. Harjo believes that memory is alive and affects the future. "I believe myth is an alive, interactive event that is present in the everyday" (Harjo 130).

The act of creating one's own personal myth is rewarding and not only connects one with their heritage but serves to provide future generations with an accurate description of a life lived within time. "I feel that any writer serves many aspects of culture, including language, but you also serve history, you serve the mythic structure that you're part of, the people, the earth, and so on—and none of these are separate" (Harjo 111). The recording of a life within history also creates us. It is through the telling of stories that we justify our emotions at any given time. "...the poem of witness must exist—because it is necessary to refresh moral life" (Muske 24). It is through the act of truth-telling testimony that we find our self, that we find our truths.

Works Cited

1.   Harjo, Joy. The Spiral of Memory Interviews. Coltelli, Laura, Editor. University of Michigan Press. 1996

2.   Muske, Carol. Women and Poetry: Truth, Autobiography, and the Shape of Self. University of Michigan Press. 1997

3.   Olney, James. Metaphors of Self: The Meaning of Autobiography. Princeton: Princeton University Press, 1972

4.   Segal, Robert A. Theorizing About Myth. Amherst: University of Massachusetts Press, 1999.

Understanding Post-Modern American Poetry

Karen Hamilton Silvestri

I had a conversation with poet and scholar, Ellen Bartlett, a few months ago. She has her own theory on when contemporary poetry took a turn from Modernism. She believes that it was when we learned to split the atom that the world of literature and arts literally exploded. Up to that point the world had a center - cities were everywhere and they were readily accessible to all with the advent of cars, roads, television, the telephone.

Following World War II, with the bombing of Japan, our center disappeared. People began to move outward from the cities and into newly created suburbs. Women did not wish to return to the world of housekeeping after tasting the freedom of war-time employment. Minorities also felt the impact of a newly found freedom. We split the atom, the center of everything, and in so doing we created chaos. The Contemporary Poets reflect this chaos.

The characteristics of Post-Modern Poetry include many modernist themes and many modernist themes taken to new levels. The largest indicator of Post-modern poetry is the "absence of a single dominant style" (Norton 2649) . Other characteristics include, "Mix of image with narrative, mix of image with discursive, precise observation, philosophical reflection, open-ended juxtaposition, multiple stories, alterations in Point of View, digressions, no coherence or closure, and unexpected jumps & disjunctive thinking" (Norton 2647). There is also "an apprehension of the invisible world, fragmentation" (Norton 2646) , and a style that appears to be a "poetic diary or journal" (Norton 2646).

Language as emotion

Language can name the pain but it can't be the pain, language cannot reach the actual individual feeling.

Christ-like in its simplicity and complexity, poetry brings the reader one stop closer to seeing their world just a little deeper. (me)

Metapoems are poems about how poems and language operate. They have no fixed center, it is "a hymn to possibility" as John Ashbery says.

The reality you are experiencing is your emotional state at any given time. We respond to our interpretations of what happens, not what has happened. This gives you an emotional state, an emotional state that reinforces and affects interpretation that in turn affects emotions.

How do you articulate the nothing? Something is there and then suddenly it is gone. Language is not strong enough. What needs to be conveyed is so horrific and deep that it is difficult for the average person to comprehend or if they can they draw back from the intensity of it.

Paul Celen: "poem, the noem" (In German means "gedicht, das genicht", which translates to 'poem, not poem') In other words, "poem negated".

As we translate the material world into words we change the material world.

John Berryman uses confessional and theatrical poetry. His syntax is contorted and reveals a sense of agony. These irregularities are balanced by strict six-line stanzas. He utilizes imaginary characters.

Gwendolyn Brooks uses irregular lines and sudden rhythm. Hers is one of passionate observation that expresses love and rage.

Fragmentation

It is interesting to note that Modern Poetry laments loss and fragmentation, while Post-Modern Poetry celebrates it. There are notions of whole fragments that don't link to any conclusion. Anne Lauderbach suggests that as our lives are made up of strings of fragments, so is post-modern poetry. Coherence is the falsehood. If we insist on neatness we will leave out something of significance - too neat is false, you experience nothing. Fragments create variety (Lauderbach).

John Ashbery uses wild and witty imagery with organized details that create nature rather than imitate it. His diction is manipulated and he uses unexpected juxtapositions.

Adrienne Rich seeks to break out and create a dialogue of self and soul. She discovers and projects dramatic situations through fragmented and confessional language.

Interpretation

In interpreting Modern Poetry you take from a poem what you need to take, which may not be what the writer intended but that is okay because you take the feeling, you get in touch with the emotion. To paraphrase John Ashbery, "You, the reader, add the flowers to the field with your interpretation." The poet creates an openness, an empty field and the reader connects with the emotion and fills the field with fragments, creating a whole.

The Modern Poets are teaching us to see the world in different ways than we are used to.

Readers have to learn to dance to the new music.

Poems are about how language works as well as subject and content. A poem is not a puzzle to be solved but an experience, an event to take part in.

Order vs. chaos

Anne Lauderbach says, "Depart from the tune - breaking the form is the form. We explore the world through forms" (Lauderbach). Creating a dyad, what is unfamiliar is outside, what is familiar is inside.

Works Cited:
1. Lauderbach, Anne. Notes from Lauderbach's lecture at Florida Atlantic University, Boca Raton, Florida, 1/30/01

Poems

Merlene Fawdry

Merlene Fawdry lives in rural Victoria, Australia. She enjoys the diversity of writing poetry, nonfiction and fiction and provides an editing, manuscript preparation and mentoring service for other writers. She has a strong interest in social justice and is committed to giving a voice to the oppressed through her writing.

Find out more about Merlene at:
https://www.facebook.com/pages/Merlene-Fawdry/258877674131384
http://merlenefawdry.blogspot.com.au/
https://twitter.com/merlenepoet
http://www.linkedin.com/profile/view?id=2763 4411&trk=nav_responsive_tab_profile_pic

Even Here

Merlene Fawdry

Even here, in this place,
Where pedestrians move
Anonymously, down glittered malls
Of enticement, piped music
Subliminally suggesting, lulling shoppers
Into a false sense of must-have

Even here, where mirrored balls
Reflect and magnify temptation
And blinkless orbs observe
Every rushing movement,
The caring of big brother
Monitored dispassionately

Even here, where crowds push
Down stall-littered halls
The touch of strangers
Unfelt beneath the skin
While aloneness shrieks
From hunched shoulders
Of vacant eyes

For grief cannot be consoled
By encounters with strangers
Nor tempted by the bling of impulse,
Or razzle dazzle of fake festivity
For sorrow is at its deepest, even here
In this heartland of the living

Once

Merlene Fawdry

Once,
in a time
before aging became
a status, scorned
by society, intent
on stretching youth
into middle age
and beyond,
life stories could be traced
in the beauty
of hills and furrows
on faces of the aged

tales of happiness
radiating as a joyful sun
from corners of eyes
to console
sadness tugging
at the side of a smile

once,
faces spoke the truth
of life
each crease and crevice
a bookmark
for the chapters of time

once,
in a time
before
memoir
turned to fiction

Always

Merlene Fawdry

Please stay with me as twilight falls
On the longest, darkest night
Sit by my side and comfort keep
Till the coming of the light.

Dress my face in brightest smile
To farewell the ones I love
And to greet the great creator
On my recall to above.

Allow not the veil of tears to cleanse
The essence of my being
Nor overwrite the man I was
For truth is in the seeing.

And whence we part in coming dawn
Let sunlight fill your days
For I, held fast within your heart
Will walk with you, always.

Tanya Fernbank

Tanya Fernbank is a 42-year-old English Language (EFL) teacher with an MA in English Lit. She spent many years working abroad and is interested in writing from around the world. She tends to write about things that annoy her in a humorous way. She has had several poems published by *United Press* (including 'The Girl with no Skirt' and 'Friends Like These, as well as and one by *Forward Poetry*. She also submits to some online sites. Her interests include theatre, travelling, painting and yoga.

Fare You Well, Welfare

Tanya Fernbank

I'd like to state
The welfare state
Seems far from well or fair
I fear;
The system on my nerves does grate
It's well unfair in this fair state
Do *you* fare well in this state?

Are you fully aware of this woolly affair?
Welfare's a fair
A lucky dip to afford your fayre;
The welfare in a state of decay,
Unfare and unwell-
I'm afraid it's 'Fair You Well, Welfare'

Andrew J. Goggans

Andrew J. Goggans is a professional medical writer and freelancer in the Raleigh, NC area. He enjoys devoting his time to various writing endeavors and life with his wife and three lovely daughters. Described by friends as a "modern hobbit," Andrew records his efforts, adventures, and contemplations at:
andrewjgoggans.com
skippingbachelorhood.wordpress.com.

The Hibernian
Andrew J. Goggans

The Moon smiles at me like Chester the Cat.
A drag on my pipe, a puff of smoke later,
I smile right back as I tip my hat.
"Another Sweet Josie," I tell the waiter.
I scribble, setting slip'ry thoughts solid.
Like ocean waves inside I ride my buzz.
Writing a record of all that I did,
All that I thought and felt the world was.
In Luna's light I write in deep delight.
The noisy pub, the greasy grub, only add
To the wellspring of words that fit just right.
A night all to myself thoroughly had.

Humbled Anew

Andrew J. Goggans

I often wonder,
I so often muse,
After I blunder
And my way thus lose,
Or "My will!" thunder
And Thy love abuse,
How Thou doth show me
Exactly where and
How I so failed Thee.
A touch from Thy hand
Bends my stubborn knee,
Shows me childish, and
Doth wholly suffice
To melt my hard heart
And make me realize
Just how great Thou art.

Trudging On

Andrew J. Goggans

Deep to my soul it clings,
A wordless thought I cannot speak
A heavy tangle of feelings
Which I've wrestled for many a week.
As verbose as I can be,
Still my tongue fails me.

It's not quite depression
That eats and eats away in me:
A pent up frustration
Oh so slowly poisoning me.
It sickens to the bone
as I struggle

alone.

Kathleen Kline

Kathleen Kline lives in Tehachapi, California. Kathleen has been purposely playing with words for over 22 years. She added a formal Journalism education to her self-started wordsmithing work years ago and enjoys helping other writers make sure what they have written is clearly expressed. Her goal is to effectively communicate while writing well crafted ditties.

http://kathleensdragonflydesk.wordpress.com/
TheHandMaiden_Kathleen@hotmail.com

Invisible but a Monster
Kathleen Kline

I fear the monster that has been lingering in
the shadows.
It is a complex and toxic monster.
Is it an ordinary monster?
My story is not unlike others out there.
It has, undeniably, caused my movements to
become slow and purposeful,
Lethargic, Sloth-like.
There are times I struggle putting one foot in
front of the other.
But struggle I do.
I will honor my responsibilities.
I will honor my gift.
No matter that I feel the monster creeping up
on me.
The monster looms ever nearer to thee.
I have decided to walk, one foot in front of the
other, even though I would like to run,
I hope I have made the right decision.
I do not have the strength to fight much more.
I feel the monster it is laying in waiting.
I fear it will consume me.
The visits come more frequently.
And I feel the loss of self ... looming, like a
stalker in the night.
I push the monster away, but it is getting
stronger.

I am faltering under its tenacity.
As I fall on bent knees I pray I do not implode.
I feel it trying to take over.
I pray the monster does not win, but fear it
will.

Moments of Weakness That Linger

Kathleen Kline

When the frustrations drip from the corners of
your eyes
When the body's communication is speaking
Greek to you
When rest does not release the demons
plaguing you
You beg for more
More time
More understanding
More guidance
More grace
Less cramping
Leas uncertainty
Less confusion
Less fatigue

The Hunted
Kathleen Kline

Sometimes I find myself avoiding
The sleeping in my own room
Sometimes avoiding sleeping all together
As if it will help me,
Help me to stave off the truth.
Yet nights and days, like today,
The truth follows me
Like a bold hunter
With a near-starving family to feed.
Whether awake or asleep
I can not deny what I know.
As much as I try.
But momma's gonna try anyways
As the tears sting my eyes
Raw the skin around them, again.
May your visits ease all of our hearts
As I know you visit more than just me.
I will come home, as you asked of me this
week
But not just yet Lovie.
More toiling to do down here on Earth,
But thanks for the invite.
I love you too.

Nicholas McKay

Nicholas McKay lives in the western suburbs of Melbourne, Australia, and is currently undertaking a post-graduate Masters course in creative writing, publishing and editing from Melbourne University. He is an online journalist and student ambassador, and has a fondness for technology. He enjoys intellectual conversations, old English love poetry and advocating mental health awareness. In his spare time, when he is not being a video gaming geek, Nicholas writes poetry and prose on his blog, which can be found at the following link:
http://totalovrdose.wordpress.com/

Origin

Nicholas McKay

The origins of my poetic verse
within my lip-synced mind,
smile like daffodils on the
beaches of Normandy; a
memoriam to the fallen
effigies of my creation which
were, alas, sacrificed to
embolden my endeavours,
now straining to stay afloat
after the fear of drowning in
my sub-conscious. The first
poem which ever did pass my
fingertips to the page,
defaced with the worries of a
depressed mind who speaks
in soliloquy, did so gently
from the heart of my writing
passions. But now the tide
has gone back out into the
deepest, darkest recesses of
my once humbled ocean's
crevasse, and threatens to
remain submerged until I can
resurrect the spark which
initiated my journey. The
inner sarcophagus of my

mind trapped within a body
of youthfulness, paralyses
the floundering membranes
of these hands as I attempt
to construct comprehensive
verse. Every word which
fails to abide with my
original integrity only assists
with digging my imagination's
immortal grave, which I have
unfortunately become too
comfortable in, slumbering
on the jagged rocks where I
have lain before. When this
deep inside the abyss of a
long suffering poet's fault
stricken mind, attempting to
pluck the ripest fruits of a
potential verse, is the only
method worth considering
towards Heaven's ascendancy
and away from undisrupted
turmoil, but the painful risks
of corroded decadency are as
plausible in equilibrium as
my literary salvations.

Sorry does not Justify Written Woe

Nicholas McKay

In a time like this, apologies are as
meaningless
as a sun within a storm, the howling gusts of a
tempest so terrifying it frightens the Heavens
away, being no place for the burning embers
of
our nearest star. If only there was but a
moment
when I could glide upon a torrential breeze,
and fly beyond the cloud cover towards where
the purest blue of the aquatic sky becomes
the
deepest shade of our black stratosphere, I
would never need to speak the words which
would grant me with forgiveness, for never
would the eyes of thee ever fall upon mine
again. Could my sinful nature really be so
cruel, as to earn the wrath of a punishment,
the ramifications of which words could barely
comprehend? Cannot a simpler conclusion
validate the once youthful feelings which
cascaded across the plateaus that ran
throughout our minds, synchronised by a
connection more endearing than romanticism
itself? What we once shared however it

seems has been heinously razed to the ground, and no manner of excuses will ever promptly justify that which ended with much disapproving woe, the briefest of serene engagements.

To Someone who Once Loved me

Nicholas McKay

To spend the night alone,
quietly contemplating, is
to spend the night an
absentee of the world.
Whilst many a man would
proclaim 'bring out the
ladies!', I deny myself
the satisfaction of alluring
company in exchange for
a lacking paradise of
intense animosity. My
fated existence brought
me to the forefront of a
loneliness so
unfathomable, it defies all
known comprehension,
and to that I drink a glass,
or twelve, of the least
expensive white wine, in
the hopes of drowning
my ever lacklustre self-
esteem. You relinquished
the pedestal I applied you
to, banishing every
moment we spent
together from the arteries

of your palpitating
romance when your
unfinished life fled the
world. What choices still
exist today, when the
hands of inebriated
violators are able to
employ all decisions that
are cast upon ourselves,
and in but a moment,
murder the seeds of
happiness which were but
an inch from sprouting. If
human life is so precious,
why is it so easy to
eradicate, and why more
so are the orchestrators of
tragedy able to forget so
easily by succumbing to
the simple act of taking
the creator's name in vain?
All around, the ashes of
integral relationships
flounder in the breeze,
and I cannot help but
wonder why those who
perpetrate much evil end
life with such a loving
smile, whilst I, a man
with a futile place in the
fields of aggression, am
forced to weep in

solitude? Perhaps I ought
to by now remove the
sign proclaiming that your
ghost is welcome here,
for only in life were you
the cause of my illustrious
salvation, and now you
bring only dismay to an
already gloomy soul
cursed with unforgotten
sorrow. To say 'goodbye'
is the last thing I could
ever want, but maybe I
am in fact instead crying
out the words 'hello, can
you hear me' into a world
which has been without
my voice that was buried
beneath silence's
silhouette for far too long.

Bob McNeil

Bob McNeil recalls, at the age of six, <u>A Child's Garden of Verses</u> planted a seed in his mental soil. Now, since the Autumn of Adulthood has descended upon him, Mr. McNeil feels his harvest came in the form of a position as Poetry Editor for BLACFAX and the publication of his two books. Both of these poetic compositions, <u>Secular Sacraments</u> and <u>The Nubian Gallery, A Poetry Anthology</u>, can be found in various libraries, universities and bookstores.

Bob McNeil was influenced by the Imagists and the Negritude Movement. Furthermore, even after all these years of being a professional illustrator, spoken word artist and writer, he still hopes to express and address the needs of the human mosaic.

Besides writing professionally, Bob McNeil is an orator of some renown. For example, he was the Featured Poet at numerous libraries throughout the tri-state area. He looks forward to performing again with his spoken word and music group in the future.

Kindly refer to Facebook, mcneil_bob@yahoo.com or YouTube for more information about poems, songs and videos. If you prefer postal mail, Bob McNeil can be reached at P.O. Box 144, Hollis, NY 11423.

A Versified Voyage

Bob McNeil

Another boy was raised at the Hudson River
   With a firm Earth Sign—
   A promising limb on an African tree—
   And The Thinker, his archetype,
   Sat beneath his unburdened brow.
24 seasons later,
   The child scrutinized
   The Lost Tribe's Jerusalem—Harlem.
   And Like East 127th Street's Shakespeare,
   Langston Hughes,
   The boy embraced his race.
At 54 seasons,
   The boy became a knowledge-consuming
entity
   Learning about African-rhythmic prose,
odes,
   Bantu, Zulu, Malinke, Yoruba,
   South of the Sahara songs.
The child traveled
   The geography of his mentality
   With David Diop, Dadie,
   Césaire and Senghor,
   Poets who created the seeds
   That became Afrocentric Breeds.
To the boy,
   These poets were sight-igniting keys.
   By plying those keys,

He opened doors to vistas
Where Black people were birthing
A renown-bound future.
Eluding adult's brimstone-sizzling stress,
Beneath a dirt-antiquated tree,
He studied comfortably
And saw the spirits of the pundits.
At 55 seasons,
With his ever-present pen and paper,
He was runner-in-a-race-inspired—
Those were his sight-igniting keys.
By plying those keys,
The child and a page converged
And an aged griot emerged.

sword of words

Bob McNeil

we create
we shape
we mold
a cosmos of star-lustered concepts with words
God-hallowed words
sage-made words
Adam-ancient words
sermon-mounting words
we write
we inspect
we dissect
exposing our love-housing hearts
exposing our world-impaired spirits
we infuse each page with words
passion-inclined words
birth-painful words
war-morbid words
rainbow-garnished words
the serum, language
flows from our veins
words are forces
possessing an artery
to assault or soothe
we're poets
throughout our souls
throughout our limbs
we feel our poems

Our parts of which we speak
Bob McNeil

I enjoy the way your verbs
    taste, stroke and titillate
    my hut of flesh and its resident soul.

I endure the way your adjectives
    desire to describe the details of beauty.
    Adjectives are paintings of dawn:
    they strike sulphur,
    but they do not emblazon my vision with
brilliance.

I revere the nouns that name
    the person, place and thing that you are.
    Every appellation I use provides
    another reference to the benevolence of
you.

I hate the pronouns assigned to design
ourselves,
    for enwrapping yourself in pink
    won't disguise the cries of your mannish
side
    and my anima is pregnant with a passion to
reproduce.

I appreciate the conjunction that you have
grown to be.
   You are the "And" that facilitates my spirit's
state
   By using the adhesion of compassion.

I adore you for the prepositions that grant
these facts:
   I am on a bed of beatitude with you.
   We do what we want for joy's geysers,
   experiencing satisfaction after the flow.

I titter at the interjections
   we use as illustrations of our jubilation.
   The exclamations are sillier
   than children chortling on a carousel.

 I assert adverbially,
   both you and I have become
   rather pledged to the notion
   of cherishing an emotion
   without using its word.
   Soundlessly appreciating that thoughtful
space,
   waiting for language to transport the topic,
   our best sentiments on commitment are
expressed.

Mairi Neil

Mairi Neil founded the Mordialloc Writers' Group 20 years ago and still coordinates the community writing group.

She also teaches creative writing in neighbourhood houses. She says she can't imagine a day when she is not writing or reading, or thinking about words.

Visiting Singapore 1973
Mairi Neil

We crowd on deck as the cruise ship glides
into Singapore harbour, a week after leaving
Fremantle.
The silver sun aglow in a cloudless azure
sky. Skin fiery scarlet from too many hours in
the ship's pool
as Singapore City wobbles and wilts in the
heat.

I ache for relief
from this tantalising veil
and covet the sea

Engines thrum and screeches of gulls mask
the first hint a change is on the way.
Rain falls in sheets and shafts. Solid blocks of
water pound the decks.

Clouds scud across sky
The veil now a fog blanket
Hiding the city.

Beneath our feet racing rivers fill deck gutters
and our shoes. On automatic pilot,
we slosh for cover, although there is no icy
wind in this downpour.

No unsettling chill
Just instant relief
From relentless heat

Rain hammers metal, swamps furniture and
people, drenching everything not covered.
Metal rails hiss. Steam sizzles on the shrinking,
not sinking ship. No crevice escapes.
A continuous stream of trickles and dribbles
demonstrates the power of this deluge.

A turmoil of grey
Idyllic tropics in grip
Of monsoonal rain

Yet, within minutes, the ship docks and the
downpour stops as quickly as it began.
Singapore City a perfect watercolour painting
showcases sunlight and serenity.
The tropical shower and haze but a dream as
perspiration leaks from every pore.

Grief.

Shelter from the storm

Mairi Neil

Bruised clouds sweep the sky
a gloomy ominous pall.
I remember your voice
'*a thunderplump is on its way.*'

Nearing sixty,
I wish to be six again
to feel comforting arms
gather me close.

Cushioned against your chest
my anxious heart
working overtime
Pit pat pit pat pit pat

Until attuned to your
gentle breathing, and steady
ba boom ba boom
ba boom.

To relax, as your hands
usually burdened with chores
keep me safe
in rhythmic caress.

Taken for a Ride
Mairi Neil

Saturday morning no school - hurrah!
Cold linoleum surprises bare feet,
but outside,
concrete path toasty warm.
Dappled sunlight shimmers as
jasmine clings to verandah posts,
and tiny rays dance on
the honeysuckle leaves
oozing sweetness and
hugging dilapidated fence.

Long grass trembles
at the Clydesdale's swishing tail.
The milk horse
waiting… waiting…
Full bottles clink,
and empties slip into crates
Eight pints
left beneath the letterbox
the only shade
from a curdling heat.

Halters jangle
grit swirls
the horse shakes its head,
snorts, and snickers.
We are the last delivery.

The milkman nods
and I scramble onto the cart.
'Home James,' he commands,
showing off
reins loose across overalled knees.

Dust scatters from the unmade road
teases nostrils and eyes
the cart creaks,
bottles and hooves
clatter and thud.
The five-minute
bone-shaking ride
to Croydon Dairy
more thrilling
than Luna Park's Big Dipper.

Why Write?

Mairi Neil

What motivates people to put pen to paper?
In writers' groups, and creative writing classes
people reveal much more than words -

A has aspirations to write a novel

B likes to play with words

C has a loveless life and seeks romance

D thinks Mills and Boon absurd

E loves family history

F reads and journals a lot

G creates settings with descriptive flair

H just loves to plot!

I preaches grammar absorbed from school

J admits to being a hopeless speller

K always suffers from writer's block

L is an expert storyteller.

M adores purple prose

N employs similes galore

O aches to be published one day

P escapes household chores

Q uses metaphors imaginatively

R nurtures the inner child

S writes for children while libertarian

T is erotica gone wild

U is definitely a poet

V writes doggerel and verse

W fears rejection

X is tense and terse

Y dramatises everything producing
performance pieces to entertain
and **Z** – well -

Z needs to write to share emotion - the
musings society's gain!

Leaves fall in autumn

Everywhere

And the trees become bare and

Very sad through winter until an

Early bud heralds

Spring!

The Mirror
Mairi Neil

(after Sylvia Plath)

Why do you challenge me every morning? Do
you think muted morning light will make a
difference to the harsh incandescence of
nightly fluorescents? Your eyes seek what I
cannot give. I cannot stop you turning into
your mother, or give you back your youth. I
cannot heal the surgeon's scar; replace the
slice that changed your life.

I know you think I'm fickle. You rub to polish
my view, seek a clarity I cannot give. It may
make me reflect more clearly your desires, but
not reality. A trick of the light your excuse as
those once bright eyes mist and dull. I cannot
control your heart or mind. I tell it how it is for
me. I may be silver-coated but not silver-
tongued.

But, why believe me? Does my opinion matter?
I cannot reach out into the world, engage with
people the way you can. Take well-worn
advice, *seek and ye shall find*. There's a
window to your soul only you can unlock, and
change is constant. Don't challenge me

because my view will always be limited. My
reflections dependent upon light.

My power is gifted - take it back.

Trinity Renee'

TrinityRenee describes herself as "Thinker, inventor, writer, tiny tyrant, audio engineer, programmer, dancer, business owner, philanthropist, singer (used loosely, should read "Shower performer"), painter, sister, friend, pet owner, daredevil, comedienne, cover stealer and the list goes on and on. But, most importantly, I am a Learner. I believe life is to live, so I try to explore as many avenues of it as possible. In short, my true biography should only state."

Trinity   Renee',   Life   Long   Learner
| TrinityRenee.com

These poems were previously published in *Reflections: A Ripple in Still Water*.

Canvas: A Thousand Words

Trinity Renee'

Sweet scent fills the air
I turn swiftly
Almost certain of it's owner
Never have I smelled such an intoxicating
scent

The aroma of you fills this room
Intimate cuddling
Giggles of contentment
Candid moments of harmony
Just you

I move through the passages of life surviving
But you still manage to find ways to remind
me
Of things I long to forget, but secretly nurture

I breathe in once more
Making sure to make a mental note
Not like I'd forget
I remember everything about you

Your Smile,
Making my heart swell every time it played
upon your face
Convincing me that through it, truths of love
Paint themselves real

Your Eyes,
Honest beauty
Displaying vivid images of happiness and
passion
Selling nothing but unspoken dreams and
fervent devotion

Your Voice,
Seemingly speaking symphonies of country
meadows
And lazy Sundays
Warming every part of me in search of the one
thing
It speaks directly to

Your Kiss,
Expressing desire in its rawest form
Giving soft declarations of unabashed bliss
Forever existent on mine as conscious
memory

Lastly
Your Mind,
The sexiest thing about you and the hardest
to forget
The purest carbon copy of exceptional
Harboring ideals of intimacy
in the most innocent of settings
Proving unconditional true
time and time again

A picture's said to say a thousand words,
and the words
are never the same
well I pray this poetic portrait of you says only
one

Love

Only With You (Let Me Dream With You)

Trinity Renee'

Let Me Dream With You
I know I have my fair share of crazy
and you
an abundant supply of stubborn but
Can I dream with you?

I have thoughts that keep me up at night
plaguing my mind with what ifs and why not
right nows
having so much to prove and so much to be
I'm never sure whether the direction I'm
headed in
is the place I'm supposed to be but
Can we dream together?

You never had a role model you could put
your finger on
so now everything you do is to show how
much you've grown
You don't need anyone or anything
You're headstrong and determined to provide
stability
always knowing exactly where you wanted to
be but
Can you dream with me?

We argue about all the ways we can fail in life
bringing up matters closest to the heart
always making sure we feel the sting
but I always believe you when you say you
love me
not because in that moment I believe it's true
but I'm always certain, when we argue
I feel that passion you have for me
even when we disagree
Do your dreams include me?

I'm always second guessing my purpose
citing chance and luck as my greatest foes
never once trusting that fate has only great
things in store
proving faith the nemesis of my dreams
but you believe in me and that fills all the
spaces that I need
Say you'll dream with me.

You take me to the places that make up the
you
I fell in love with
Sharing more than I could ever ask for but
desire all the same
telling me stories of why I'm perfect
and how you couldn't Dream of doing this
with anyone else
getting down on one knee and asking me
to be the first piece in a vision we could share
together
for the rest of our lives

Can we dream for two?

Long days, endless nights and pleasant
surprises
Laying here in your arms is still my preferred
choice
You ask me if I ever dreamed this life shared
could feel so complete
I take in all of life's lessons and place them
against your resilience and my love
understanding that the mixture of both made
this life true
My answer
No, Only With You

We, The Willing
Trinity Renee'

We, The Willing,
led by the unknowing
are doing the impossible
for the ungrateful...

Timothy L. Rodriguez

Timothy L. Rodriguez was a journalist when newspapers counted, he is a poet when poetry doesn't count for much, and he is a novelist when the fate of fiction is uncertain. He has published in English and Spanish. His most recent novel, *Guess Who Holds Thee?*, is available on Amazon. He makes loose change selling his seascapes. He is a practitioner of Robert's Frost's line—the only certain freedom is in departure; he has travelled widely and assumed many walks of life. For the moment he lives on a barrier island in North Carolina where he learns humility by surf fishing and golf.

Guess Who Holds Thee?
Timothy L. Rodriguez

At the River

Timothy L. Rodriguez

The talk in the office
is that the sky said
to the rain—Leave.

Now I hear that time,
the rowdy version,
told promise—Come off it;

as if a silly pretense,
a suckle for dreambangers,
a tryst for daylight doubters,
a vista for talent timers.

Scarcely can I believe
how cock the command—
Come off it! Is it a slight,
a chide or just a demand?

I recognize how promises
tend to story like storms.
They pass through seasons
holding out wondrous forms.

But promises are pushers;
first one's free but facedown.
They deliver moments too late,
only their betrayals 're on time.

Promises revolve, seasons
turn, and we the hapless ones
spin in unwanted winds.

Now I heard the word
Is that the church
told the fold—Gather

Ailene Rogers

Ailene Rogers is a mother of 4, a retired science teacher, biologist, environmentalist, and part of the Taproots writing group out of SUNY, Stonybrook

The Pace of a New Age

Ailene Rogers

My rhythm is different
    From what it used to be.
It is so much slower
    But that's how it must be!
I can't jog as swiftly
    When I go on walks.
I don't respond quickly
    To other peoples' talks.
When I do forget
    My current condition,
I put myself
    In an awkward position.
So I keep experimenting
    Taking a risk,
Playing it too slowly
    Then making it too brisk!
When I am too slow
    I become impatient.
When I am too fast
    I work with hesitation.
If I don't find my way
    My heart has palpitations.
So I must seek
    New recreations.

It's hard to be flexible
    To see things anew.

Communion, time, and nature
     Bring another view.
A service at church
     With friendly greetings;
Brings new courage
     And new meetings.
A quiet time with Steve
     Snuggling and sharing
A chat, a complaint
     Then deep caring,
An email from a friend
     With a clever quoted line,
A call from the children
     Saying they're all fine,
An Indian summer day
     In early November
All give me the chance
     To discover a new temper.
The scene from the bridge
     With sun, swans and geese,
Shows reflections in the pond,
     Brings images of peace,
Quelling insecurities
     Of all the sudden changes
Accompanying this greater age
     Of slackened tempo ranges!

First Snow

Ailene Rogers

(With acknowledgement to Stanlee Lonsdale, my first college roommate who wrote of "A Snowflake" as a gift for my 18th birthday, January 17, 1960)

A cold change is in the air
    Lightly dusting ground, leaves, needles.
Not a squirrel, bird, chipmunk even stirs
    Making all white and serene
On a gray day
    Portending further changes ahead.

I water houseplants
    Now safely ensconced
Carry the few last stragglers in
    Secured and warm
Will they bloom again?

What is that special silence
    That surrounds
The gently covered world?

Snowflakes fall without a sound
    Blocking noises from around
A quiet curtain of lacy grace and peace.

November 12, 2013

Flights of Fantasy
(The Promise of another chance at life)
Ailene Rogers

We flew South eight hundred miles
     To celebrate a family Easter.
Midst all the renewal of love
     And festival of joy
We came into summer
     Warm green shaded and blossomed.
Then returned north
     To the season of daffodils and forsythia.
No longer did leaves shade
our way,
We experienced spring again.
Perhaps we might go north still further
     To our younger years
To revisit lost loved ones
     Recapture vernal youth.
If by travel you can live a season
     Twice within a year,
Why not revisit earlier
     Life and companions dear?
But maybe this is truly what
     The celebration of Easter is?
The promise of another chance at life!

Susan Skvorc

A Temporary Torment

Susan Skvorc

In the chair the sights are limited.
Without a mirror I am blind.
Sounds and smells and touch are dominant
Painting visions in the mind.

Hands encased in smoothest blue,
Black hairs curling at the cuffs,
Hover inches from my eyes.
Reminding me I hate this stuff.

The fear descends, the body tenses,
A sheet of green is draped across
And anchored firmly as defense
Against potential fluid loss.

With vision useless, eyes are closed.
The tongue, half dead, can feel it all.
The rubber block between the teeth
Allows the hands to scale the wall.

The ears at once become alert,
A whining, whirring serpent creeps.
Its cry announces its assault,
Inside, with no apology, it leaps.

A single fang of steel spins round,
While bits of armor, yielding, fly

Into the air. The smell of bone
Alarms the nose, I cannot lie.

All the senses on high alert,
Unpleasant sounds transmit through bone.
My jaw fatigued from staying open,
The serpent's cry becomes my own.

Its whine declines, its writhing ceases.
The rubber dam comes out.
My heart is whole, my tooth in pieces,
The space around it filled with grout.

And now I see the hands of blue.
My elevated stress slides down,
To rise again in seven days,
For this is not the final crown.

Enzo Silvestri

Enzo Silvestri was born in Torrice, Italy and grew up in Queensland, Australia. He works as an English instructor at Fayetteville Technical Community College and East Bladen High School. He holds a BA in English and History, a B.Ed in Italian and English, and an MA in Applied Linguistics.

Enzo is the author of *The Fig Tree, Rock of Ages, Thief in the Night, The Caver King*, and *The Time Card Series* (juvenile literature).

silven@live.com
www.karenzomedia.net
http://enzosilvestri.wordpress.com/
http://timecardseries.wordpress.com/

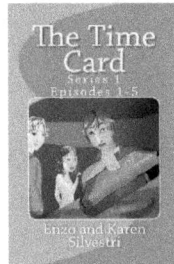

A Punny Foem

Enzo Silvestri

For Sallyanne

In elegance they wrote
Penned 'em a poem
To the reader is quote
And mostly they know 'em
The poet's a phantom
With pictures and words
Chooses at random
Did she eat curds

Little miss Muffet
That's her name
Sat on a tuffet
What's her game?
In came the spider
Went for the dregs
Sat down beside her
RACK OFF HAIRY LEGS!

Now to write an ode
One needs some wit
To walk on a Toad
Could get you a zit
If it don't rhyme
It still can be funny
And if you got time
Why not make some money

Started now the mystery
Who coined this game
A Mayor of recent history
That'd be her name

4 - May – 1993

Blind Confusion

Enzo Silvestri

"You can't, you can't! You just can't preach!
We don't want to hear about God all the time."
So is heard whene'er one tries to reach
Thro' self-delusion, whose open eyes are blind

Telling them, smiling-yes, they heard it all
"So the past is past, now we live for now."
But little is known of how He stops the fall
"Everlasting life!" they say, "How, just how?"

His name it is Power, the Glory, the Most High
Embraced by all, yes, everyone who asks
Whenever needed His presence is nigh
Wit Joy and Peace, and help in all tasks

Standing at the door, knocking at the heart
Waiting to enter, to give life anew
From year dot, like a brand new start
If the mouth shall confess the words so true

Critics say that preaching is antiquated out
Did He not say in parting, "Go teach them all."
How, but by teaching, is one cleared of doubt

Yes how can one see, yet ne'er hear His call

By loving now His wish is to reconcile
That all be saved, and know what is true
For the sinner is loved, the sin is bile
Call on His name, join His saving queue

26 - December - 1978

The Sower

Enzo Silvestri

*One thing I know, that, whereas I was
blind, now I see.* (John 9:25)

A sower went out in the field one day,
The seeds he sowed he threw 'em all around.
He sowed good seed wherever they fell,
and the good fruit came from the good ground.
Some of them fell on the path in between,
Some of them fell on soil full of rock,
Others fell and grew among thorns,
But the good ones brought forth plenty stock.

Now the world we know is the field he sowed,
But we ain't took care and it's fulla weeds.
But our eyes should always be on the sower,
He came, ploughed and planted new seeds.
Which part of the field my brother are you?
Maybe youse the track where the people walk,
Where the seed is sown and it feeds the birds.
Are you now brother no work and all talk?

Is you then like the seed on the rocks?
They done spring up but there ain't much soil,
The sun comes up and they's got no roots,
Just like him what trials will spoil.
Is you then like the seeds in thorns?
Cos when you grew, the thorns choked then,
Did your money, your honey, weigh you down,

Make you make nothing, in your world of men.

Or are you my brother on the good soil?
Bearing the fruit more'n a hundred fold,
Did you hear his word 'n' took it to y'heart?
Are you my friend, the fire-tested Gold?

18 - September 1978

Parody

Enzo Silvestri

*And other fell on good ground, and sprang up, and bare
fruit an hundredfold. (Luke 8:8)*

If you can keep y' bread, when all about you
Are losing theirs, and blaming it on you.
If you can bluff, when all men doubt you
And make allowance for their bluffing too.
If you can be calm, but not too cool
Or be debonair, a man of gambling renown
Or be smart, and pick out the fool
Yet not too sharp, just wear the crown.
If you can hustle, and not make it your boss.
If you can deal, off up or down in your game.
If you can meet with win or loss,
And still be able to keep your dame.
If you can bear to lose a valuable token
To Mr Big, and his other fools
Then take their jaws, making them all broken,
And remain as always, quite within the rules.
If you can make one heap of all your winnings
And risk it all on some sly shifty stuff
Then be called, and start at your beginnings
Winning more back, till they say "enough!"
If you force your hand with threes and pairs
Win the jackpot when they drop out
And be happy when they tear out their hairs
Saying, "You'll be the one to give me gout!"
If you can talk with Cops, keeping your cool

Or walk with babes, nor lose your sharpness,
If neither foes nor friends change your rule
If all men near you turn instantly luckless.
If you can fill the mighty jackpot
With all your chips, and win it all in won,
Yours is the Casino, and all it's got
And, which is more,
you'll be a card sharp, my son.

17 - May – 1976

Seventy-Six

Enzo Silvestri

Hopes grow dim for our land
The Headlines' booming voice is loud
And though it's not done by yours or my hand
We're still to blame, we are the crowd
Youth and loveliness slain by lust
Their memories swept away like daily dust

The tragedy occurs again and again
Our world is crying
Nightmares Devils Guerrillas Slain men
Suicides, our world is dying
People working on a single clue
Just to find they're in the same stew

Standards tumbling under economic crises
Greed and envy multiplying
All we see is ever-increasing prices
And politicians living by lying
But they say 'It's on the mend'
Could it be that we'll see the end

On the streets the children play
With toy guns and other likes
OH STOP! I'd like to say
But we teach them, we, the biggest tykes
And we're no better, our guns are real
When we say, you're dead, we don't heal

I read that Lucretia Borgia has struck again
But is she guilty or is it just her fame
No one knows, but the twelve then
Know where she goes, as she gets the blame
And the world goes living on and on
With no one caring to whence she's gone

The wrath of the unions governing all
A different strike each week
And usually arbitration will fall
raising wages to a temporary peak
I look at the world, and see the burning wicks
Finding them well lit...in seventy-six

4 - June – 1976

Festival Mania

Enzo Silvestri

The air filled with incoherent chatter
Excitement mingled happily with anxiety
Lights, throats screamed, nothing mattered
As the rising mania approached the mighty

Thoughts drowned, fans screamed in seats
Views blocked as feet mounted chairs
Countless feet tapping time to thumping beats
We were on the prowl, and gone were cares

The second stanza raised louder screams
throats parched, vendors' hollers unheard
We were jumping in a car, or so it seemed
With youth expectant of the wanted word

At last it came, he appeared
A familiar melody fills the air
Girls entering the slipstream, joyful tears
As their idol moved beneath limey glare

28 - June - 1976

Karen Hamilton Silvestri

Karen Silvestri is co-owner of Karenzo Media and an instructor of English Composition and Reading at Fayetteville Technical Community College and Robeson Community College. She currently teaches part-time and is the Instructional Specialist for the Learning Center at Robeson Community College in Lumberton, N.C. She is the author of several non-fiction books geared towards education. She enjoys art journaling and teaching memoir workshops.

karenzomedia@gmail.com

Karenzo Media www.karenzomedia.net
Hamilton Academy
http://hamiltonacademy.net/
My Altered Art
http://nonnakaren.wordpress.com/

"no climbing sitting touching or placing items on any of the walls of the Castillo"

Karen Hamilton Silvestri
from *Recuérdeme*

In the dampened portico I graze
rough stone and sharp coquina walls
a slice of past the measure of a far away star
falls to the ground – I cradle it in my palm
as I move through each darkened room
the spirits seep like smoke from the mossy
walls

remember recuérdeme

a young woman places her sparkling high
heels
on the mildewed cannon tosses
her tresses in haughty indifference,
filing her coral tipped finger
as her husband reclines on the bastion wall
castillo spirits flow through her
pressing the foot insistently

*this is all we have left y usted puso your dirty
foot on it*

here a prison cell for Osceola

dark skinned natives captured
under the white flag of truce betrayed
9 Seminole leaders, 81 warriors, countless
women and children

we only wanted to be left alone

chapel – sparkling stark holy water fonts
showing some dust of disintegration
i feel compelled to cross myself
spirits surround and press me assertively
downwards to my knees

blessusohlord la paz esté con usted hailmary
fullofgrace ourfather andalsowithyou father
son holy spirit

Note: *The Castillo de San Marcos was built in 1695 in St.*
Augustine, FL Spanish Translations: éste es mi nombre –
this is my name, puede usted oírme? – can you hear me?, y
usted puso – and, you put, la paz esté con usted- peace be
with you, recuérdeme – remember me

Cruising the Produce

Karen Hamilton Silvestri
From *The Hanging Tree*

She picks her way through the produce
aisle. Overripe bananas next to too plump
tomatoes. Melons of every size, some scarred
from birth, some damaged after leaving
the vine. Not one of them reaches perfect.
She turns

the corner and Ah! Here on this aisle is passion
(*less?*) fruit! She sighs, ditches the cart, heads
over to the candy aisle.

Samantha Stemler

Samantha Stemler is an independent author, blogger and promotional writer living in Lansing, Michigan. She self-published her first fiction novel, a teen romance entitled *That Freak Kid* in 2011 via Kindle and Nook while obtaining her bachelor's degree at Michigan State University. Her second novel, a psychological thriller entitled *The King of the Sun,* entered the e-book marketplace in December, 2013 with all proceeds benefiting the National Alliance on Mental Illness. Samantha is currently hard at work on her third novel and a collection of short stories and poetry, as well as her young and indie writer's blog, *Insidious Plot.*

samstemler@gmail.com,
Facebook.com/S.Stemler
Twitter: @samstemler
samstemler.blogspot.com
www.thekingofthesun.webs.com
www.thatfreakkid.webs.com

My Sari
Samantha Stemler

My Sari flew across the sea
Sorrowfully far from free
From deathly, fiery, dark country
Her wings drenched in agony.

She entered to our liberty
With scorn shy to intensity.
Bewildered, scarred, she hated me
And the sins of serendipity.

My Sari strode with piety
Weaved within her majesty.
And scarves of destined duty
Haloed her damnable beauty.

With eyes of biblical tragedy,
From lashes of Egyptian antiquity,
Stared the genesis of tranquility,
Glowing rapturous of eternity.

She spoke from a hilltop so softly,
Every sound such a tribute to symphony,
That the mother of light and virginity
Fawned on her smile so happily.

My Sari, the unknowable study;

A wine rose so silently lonely,
A bountiful starving anomaly,
My blessed, beautiful blasphemy.

Night shades sheltered idolatry
In devotion I dared obey.
My worship nailed to secrecy
The passion I dared not convey.

A disciple shamed to villainy,
My Goddess I worthlessly betrayed;
For, I loved her always silently—
Until God took my Sari away.

Almost Gone

Samantha Stemler

A softness like a whisper
And a whisper like a song
The only gentle words I hear
They've called me for so long.

The sun is never setting
And the night is ever drawn
The stars call out, regretting
The absence of the dawn

My lonely dark's awaiting
The moon that's long been gone
The gracious silence creating
An end to all the wrong

Pulled through hearts and longing
Regret for all I've done
Past the pain and yearning
The call is much too strong

The shadows and the reflections
The shivers in the mirrors
The fears and resurrections
Do not quaver there

The blood, the beast, the crimes;
All shall disappear
The test and trials and time;

Nothing left to fear

Where nights will dance with twilight
And the sun spills over stars
Where the stillness marries silence
And washes clean it all

Where the night will never end
And the glass will never break
Where the sun will never set
And the earth will never shake
Where the sky and earth are one
And the law of fate is done
Where time and end are gone
To the sleep of silent song

Sarah Taylor

Do You Feel Guilty

Sarah Taylor

Do you feel guilty?
For the words you said that slowly chipped
away at my self-esteem like a woodpecker
pecking at a weak tree?
For the boyfriends I lost because they can't or
won't deal with my pain?
For the small number of friends I have
because I am afraid of having more-afraid they
might be teased for my flaws?
For the physical and mental scars I bear from
where I tried to end my pain and my life?
For the times I don't eat because I fear the
word "fat" you used to throw at me with such
satisfaction was and still is true?
For the times I never even tried because I
believed that you were right when you called
me stupid?
Do you feel guilty?
I do.

Life's Puzzle
Sarah Taylor

If life is like a puzzle
Then my puzzle may never be complete.
I have so many pieces.
So many that aren't mine.
So many people give me their pieces.
So many expect me to help them complete
their puzzle.

But amidst all the other pieces I've lost my
own.
My life remains incomplete,
Jumbled,
Confused. I know I must clear my life of
puzzles that aren't mine to complete.
I must give back the pieces.
So I can find my own.

Anger
Sarah Taylor

I have an anger that burns deep inside.
I hold it down.
Can't let it loose.

I'm angry because I had to be a grown-up
instead of a child.
I'm angry because I had no one to protect me.

I'm angry because you hurt me.
I'm angry because I care.

I'm angry because you raped me.
I'm angry because I didn't fight.

I'm angry because I live with this pain.
I'm angry because you don't.

I'm angry because of all I've lost.
Because of all I'll never be.

Poetry Prompts & Exercises

Writing an Acrostic Poem
Mairi Neil

An acrostic poem is one where the first letters of the lines spell out a word or words if you read them vertically. For example, here is an acrostic poem from Lewis Carroll's *Through The Looking-Glass*, which was dedicated to Alice Pleasance Liddell. If you read the lines from top to bottom, you'll see that the first letters spell out Alice's complete name. Carroll has rhymed the lines - this is not necessary in freeform - sometimes one word suffices.

A *boat beneath a sunny sky,*
L *ingering onward dreamily*
I *n an evening of July--*

C *hildren three that nestle near,*
E *ager eye and willing ear,*
P *leased a simple tale to hear--*

L *ong has paled that sunny sky:*
E *choes fade and memories die.*
A *utumn frosts have slain July.*

Still she haunts me, phantomwise,
Alice moving under skies
Never seen by waking eyes.

Children yet, the tale to hear,
Eager eye and willing ear,
Lovingly shall nestle near.

In a Wonderland they lie,
Dreaming as the days go by,
Dreaming as the summers die:

Ever drifting down the stream--
Lingering in the golden gleam--
Life, what is it but a dream?

- Lewis Carroll

1) Write an acrostic using your name or the name of someone you love (see example)
.
2) Write an acrostic about a town or city (maybe where you were born, or a place you love to visit, dream about, or a place with special significance).

3) Write an acrostic about a season - spring, summer, autumn, or winter, - the lines spelling out the name of the season, or a particular month –– add your memories, or thoughts.

What Is An Acrostic Poem?
Mairi Neil

Definition: acrostic *a ·cros ·tic* /əˈkrôstik/
Acrostic poems are a literary composition in which certain letters in each line form a word vertically. The poem, usually in verse, has the first or the last letters of the lines, or certain other letters, in order, to form a name, word, phrase, or motto. There are many examples of acrostics in *The Bible*.

These things I have s**p**oken unto you

that in me y**e** might have peace.

in the world ye sh**a**ll have tribulation:

but be of good **C**heer;

I have overcom**e** the world.
John 16:33 and John 3:16 (King James version)

For God so **l**oved the world,

that he gave his **O**nly begotten Son,

that whosoever belie**V**eth in him should not perish,

but have ev**e**rlasting life.

The starting point of an acrostic can be yourself!

Write your name down the page and then using the letters write words or phrases across from the letters

Acrostics do not have to rhyme.

There are no rules about how long a line should be, whether just one word or a phrase.

Think about your writing aspirations and/ or personality

Mother and teacher

And a would-be novelist

It is a murder-mystery but she

Rarely gets time to write so

It will be a cold case!

Or just have fun playing with words and poetic forms!

Rapunzel, a herb, a pregnant woman craves
with insatiable appetite
And orders her husband to a neighbour's
garden, in the dead of night

Perchance the neighbour watches -- to catch the thief

Unbeknown to him, this enchantress has powers to cause grief

Not happy at the crime, she demands the babe as payment for the herb

Zealous parents agree because the cravings can't be curbed

Eventually, a girl is born, and the enchantress stakes her claim…

Longhaired Rapunzel, in a tower imprisoned, destined for fairy tale fame.

How does she escape and win freedom you may ask --
overcoming the power of an enchantress no easy task
but the main theme of a fairy tale is good versus evil
and there is much we can learn from tales medieval
consequences, promises, values of loyalty, truth, and trust
of course, LOVE frees Rapunzel - 'happy ever after' a must!

Word Search

Karen Hamilton Silvestri

The poet needs to be as surprised as the reader by the end of the poem. Let the poem surprise you." -Ezra Pound, The ABC's of Reading

This poem uses your subconscious to randomly find words that appeal to you for seemingly no reason. You will let your subconscious do most of the work as you prepare for this poem, so clear your head and prepare to let your inner you take over!

Materials Needed: old newspapers and magazines, markers

Using two very different magazines and/or newspapers, you are going on a word search. I say *word*, but actually mean that you can also search for *phrases*. With your marker, circle words or phrases that jump out at you, words that make you pause, phrases that strike you for no reason at all.

Don't think about this! Just circle every time you feel yourself pause over a word or phrase. Don't spend too much time on one page. Circle a few things then go to

the next page. Let yourself fall into a rhythm of *seeing* words but not really reading them or giving them any thought.

Do this with at least four pages from each magazine you chose. Now, go back and find the words you circled. Write them out on a piece of paper.

Once you have gathered all of your words and phrases, you are ready to begin writing your poem. You are free to add words and change tenses. You may end up not using all of the words that you circled, but be sure to give them a chance to fit in. Sometimes a word we think won't possibly work ends up tying the whole poem together!

Remember that your poem doesn't have to make complete sense, but the phrases that you create do need to have something to do with one another. We are searching for the rhythm, the music in the sounds!

Let your found words sing. You will be surprised how taking random words and phrases often leads to a quite coherent piece.

A Sample Word Search

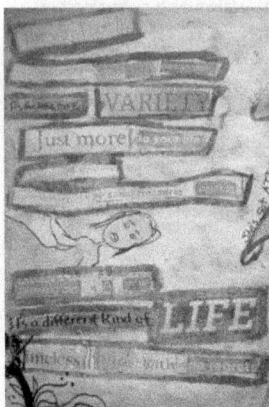

My Poem
The way I see it,
We're a pattern where life
comes together
It's the little things - variety
Just more to your life
A mix of patterned moments
Unforgettable personal
treasures waiting

Growing old is a lost art
It's a different kind of life
Timeless and with no regrets

Transform a Ballad
Enzo Silvestri

As an English teacher I have despaired of how to get students to write a ballad in the correct way. A ballad is a good tool to teach the structure of narrative writing because it has the same structure in a more visible format. This is a process that I used while teaching Foreign Lit to a 10th grade class.

1. Read some ballads (like The Geebung Polo Club below).

2. Writing a ballad may seem a daunting task, so feel free to use the worksheet included here to help you write your ballad.

3. Change the poem line by line according to where you want the story to go. For example, I was teaching Australian Ballads to American students and I used THE GEEBUNG POLO CLUB by Banjo Patterson as my template. You could use any form of narrative as a template for this purpose.

4. Take your new lines and write them together into a new ballad. The one I wrote with the class became an American ballad, THE ROBESON BASEBALL CLUB, transformed

from the original Australian classic, THE
GEEBUNG POLO CLUB. (see below)

Tips

- The ballad needn't rhyme, but a
  rhyming ballad means that more
  thought has gone into its composition.
  (refer to my quote)

- Making lines rhyme gives you the
  practice of varying your word choices
  to ensure that rhyming words end the
  lines.

- While I allowed some use of original
  themes in my transformations, be
  careful not to plagiarise someone
  else's intellectual property.

The Geebung Polo Club
Andrew Barton (Banjo) Patterson

It was somewhere up the country, in a land of
rock and scrub,
That they formed an institution called the
Geebung Polo Club.
They were long and wiry natives from the
rugged mountain side,
And the horse was never saddled that the
Geebungs couldn't ride;
But their style of playing polo was irregular and
rash —
They had mighty little science, but a mighty lot
of dash:
And they played on mountain ponies that were
muscular and strong,
Though their coats were quite unpolished, and
their manes and tails were long.
And they used to train those ponies wheeling
cattle in the scrub:
They were demons, were the members of the
Geebung Polo Club.

It was somewhere down the country, in a city's
smoke and steam,
That a polo club existed, called 'The Cuff and
Collar Team'.
As a social institution 'twas a marvellous
success,
For the members were distinguished by
exclusiveness and dress.
They had natty little ponies that were nice, and

smooth, and sleek,
For their cultivated owners only rode 'em once a
week.
So they started up the country in pursuit of sport
and fame,
For they meant to show the Geebungs how they
ought to play the game;
And they took their valets with them — just to
give their boots a rub
Ere they started operations on the Geebung Polo
Club.

Now my readers can imagine how the contest
ebbed and flowed,
When the Geebung boys got going it was time to
clear the road;
And the game was so terrific that ere half the
time was gone
A spectator's leg was broken — just from
merely looking on.
For they waddied one another till the plain was
strewn with dead,
While the score was kept so even that they
neither got ahead.
And the Cuff and Collar Captain, when he
tumbled off to die,
Was the last surviving player — so the game
was called a tie.
Then the Captain of the Geebungs raised him
slowly from the ground,
Though his wounds were mostly mortal, yet he
fiercely gazed around;
There was no one to oppose him — all the rest
were in a trance,

So he scrambled on his pony for his last expiring chance,
For he meant to make an effort to get victory to his side;
So he struck at goal — and missed it — then he tumbled off and died.

By the old Campaspe River, where the breezes shake the grass,
There's a row of little gravestones that the stockmen never pass,
For they bear a crude inscription saying,
'Stranger, drop a tear,
For the Cuff and Collar players and the Geebung boys lie here.'
And on misty moonlit evenings, while the dingoes howl around,
You can see their shadows flitting down that phantom polo ground;
You can hear the loud collisions as the flying players meet,
And the rattle of the mallets, and the rush of ponies' feet,
Till the terrified spectator rides like blazes to the pub —
He's been haunted by the spectres of the Geebung Polo Club.

The ...... Club by ....

It was somewhere ....
rock and scrub,

That they formed ....
Club.

They were ....
mountain side,

And the ....
couldn't ride;

But their style of playing ....was
irregular and rash —

They had ....
lot of dash:

And they played ....
muscular and strong,

Though their coats ....
tails were long.

And they ....
cattle in the scrub:

They were demons...............................
Club.

It was somewhere …………………………….
smoke and steam,

That a ……………..…… club existed, called
'……………………………………………. Team'.

As a social institution …………………………..
success,

For the members …………………………..
and dress.

They had natty little ………………………….
smooth, and sleek,

For ……………………………………………..
'em once a week.

So they ………………………………………….
and fame,

For they meant to show the ………………….
the game;

And they took ………………………….. to
give their boots a rub

Ere they started ………………………………..
Club.

Now my readers can imagine how …………,

When the …………………………………………..
boys got going it was time to clear the road;

And the game ………………………………..
time was gone

A spectator's leg was broken — just from
merely …………………………………………….

For they ………………………………………..
strewn with dead,

While the score ………………………… got
ahead.

And the ……………………………………………
Captain,
……………………………………………. to die,

Was the ……………………………………. tie.

Then the Captain …………………………..
from the ground,

Though his wounds …………………………
around;

By the old …………………………………….…..,
where the breezes shake the grass,

There's a row of little gravestones
……………………………….. never pass,

For they ……………………………………. a
tear,

For ……………………………………………
lie here.'

And on misty moonlit evenings,
……………………………………………..
howl around,

You can see …………………………………….
ground;

You can hear …………………………………..
meet,

And the rattle …………………………………
feet,

Till the terrified ……………………………….
to the pub —

He's been haunted …………………………….
Club.

THE ROBESON BASEBALL CLUB

Enzo Silvestri, with input from St Pauls High
Sophomores

(A transformation of "The Geebung Polo Club" by
Australian poet, A.B. (Banjo) Patterson)

It was somewhere in the county, on the flats of
swamp and scrub
That they formed a sporting group, called the
Robeson Baseball Club
They were rough and rowdy teamsmen, bred
down the Lumbee River side
And the ball was never pitched, that the Robbies
couldn't guide
But their style of playing had no plan, it was
irregular and rash
Sure, they had rough-cut bats and gloves, but a
mighty lot of dash
And they played mostly to their strengths, they
were muscular and strong
Though their uniforms had different colors, and
the folks just called 'em, wrong!
And they practiced running and turning, by
chasing cattle in the scrub
They were madmen, they were wild, were the
men of Robeson Baseball club

It was somewhere further north, in a town of
smoke and steam
That another club existed, called the
Cumberland Crusher's Team

As a social institution they were classy, and
accustomed to success
For the members had monogram'd uniforms,
and snappy pressed clean dress
They had well sewn gloves and their bats were
smooth and sleek
For they practiced on the diamond, just once
each second week
So they travelled down the I-95, in pursuit of
fortune and fame
For they meant to show those Robbies, how they
ought to play the game
Yes they took their personal butlers, just to give
their boots a rub
'Ere they started south to play, the Robeson
Baseball Club

Now my readers can imagine, how the
competition flowed
When the Robeson boys got going, it was time
to clear the road
For the game was played nine innings, or until
the time was gone
And the spectators watched in awe, from the
excitement of looking on
For the balls were thrown like bullets, soon the
field was strewn with dead
While the score remained at nil all, and no one
really got ahead
It seemed the Cumberland Crusher's captain was
the final one to die
So the umpires made a pact, and declared the
game a tie

When suddenly the Robbies' captain, raised
hisself slowly from the ground
E'en though his wounds were grave, and he was
hurting, all around
There was no one left to oppose him, so he stood
in the batter's box
He hit himself a line drive, and started hopping
like a crippled fox
For he meant to make an effort, to get victory for
his side
He ran e'en though he was done, and he scored
as he fell on home and died

Down by the old Lumber river, where the
breezes shake the grass
There's a row of little gravestones, where
Robesonians fear to pass
For they bear a crude inscription, Saying,
'Stranger, drop a tear'
For the Cumberland Crusher players and the
Robbie boys lie here
On the foggy moonlit evenings, when the
wolves they howl around
You can see the bats a-crashin', and the players
run the ground
You can hear glove and ball, make a thud
whene'er they meet
And the thumping of the runners, with ghostly
Nikes on their feet
Till the terrified run screaming, to the
Blackwater Grill Sports Pub
They been haunted by the Players of the
Robeson Baseball Club

Fragments Exercise

Karen Silvestri

Originally published as a blog post at http://ksilvestri.wordpress.com/2012/05/12/making-poems-by-using-journal-fragments/

Here is another interesting way to create poetry from your journals or memoirs. These poems are an interesting way to get at the 'meat' of your journal writing and the resulting poems can be very powerful.

If you enjoy abstract art, this type of poetry writing just might be for you. I have had amazing success with these poems. I use this form of fragment poetry with my Creative Writing classes and workshop participants.

The method:

First, agree that you will allow your thoughts to run wild! No censuring allowed here!

Browse through your journal with pen, pencil, or highlighter in hand. I personally use a pencil, so that I can go back erase the marks from my journal later. If you journal on the computer, save the journal as Fragments first, then you are free to use the highlight tool as you search through the text. Circle or highlight words or phrases that jump out of you. You are working from your gut here. Don't stop to ask why that particular word or phrase struck you, just circle it! My rule is that if I find myself pausing and pondering a word, phrase, or sentence, then I circle it.

Continue doing this for a few pages, then copy each of the circled words/phrases onto a piece of paper. I group them into lines of four to six as I copy them down... again, do not censure, just write them in the order you circled them. Read through your fragments. Now you can start moving them around. You are looking for some sort of flow here, but it doesn't have to necessarily make sense.

Continue editing by adding or deleting words. You will be surprised how the fragments need very little editing and seem to come together into a coherent piece without much editing or moving of lines!

Again, the key here is to not overthink it! Let your gut lead you and be ready for whatever jumps out at you.

Here are a couple of my fragments:

We were inseparable
Now I have some place

It keeps freezing up
All signs point to
Reality
Now it is frozen

(The above fragment came from a couple of pages of my journal and the subject matter was remembering an old friend, my computer freezing up, and what I was going to do with my day. I did no editing to that one....just wrote down the phrases that jumped out at me!)

Writing by candlelight
I am hiding
Forever on the verge of something
Always almost there
Was it all written already?
Too many questions
I don't think I'll ever get it
It is safer to stay away

* Also see *The Burrough's Cut-Up Method*

The Burrough's Cut Up Method

Sample Cut-Up Method (also called the Fold-in)
This one page piece came from three pages of journal entries. The student printed the pages, cut them up the middle vertically, then across horizontally. She then laid out the pieces on the table and randomly moved them around. Next she taped the pieces together so that she would not be tempted to interrupt the spontaneity of their random placement. She then typed the resulting document verbatim. Finally she edited the complete text by removing words, some whole sentences, and adding a word here or there for coherence. This is the narrative version; the challenge now would be to turn the narrative into a poem!

Meditative Tesserae

Went to bed at 8 or so. We watched a movie with supporting people – all more treacherous than the last. I live my own strange life. Sometimes I read back through this stuff thinking as I watch that it is very hard to think. Trying to read, record anything of value. I write about this house, it has too many people in it. I should have been one of those not afraid to share her every thought. Talking, talking, talking. I can't think straight, I know it so well that I feel like it won't come out and everyone wants to know my most private thoughts. Little old lady who holes up in her room and realizes how I don't fit in. What is she up to? Every wall covered with books. I could stay in here all day and I have. So I live books and books and books.

My topic for the day is "Make a list of...". In one section there is the night as I fall asleep. I thought it funny, I was thinking about this topic in one place and I would want to go to another. We're all alone. There's nothing. I don't want to go anywhere. My immediate thought was this crushing knowledge. We repress. I doubt I would have the energy to show how well you think you know me. I close myself off to everyone. Some people do it better than others. No one notices anyway. I have mourned the issue by filling myself with sleep. Other people just muddle me up and I realize what crap it is. At some bizarre time, all my defenses will crumble and I will have been reading too much Neitscze.

How quickly I rush in to cover myself. The book, scarcely pausing to explain meaning in life...why bother? If you live you can see that people have always believed. But I don't think it will be a good choice of books for covering the point. But that is our topic. To live here we call this Higher Power God out by writing on loose-leaf paper. This just sent me reeling further down into the inadequacies of organized religion. The Native Americans had no organized Great Spirit. I am sick to death of trying to help.

Messenger turned off – it is just me. Where is your favorite place to hide? Is it possible for us to be alone? In a little place always gravitating towards dark corners - to my books and my writing. I know that I need to recreate my life and start over. But I don't think that will do a damn thing. Characters say "You don't know how to read to me." How do we deal with our minds these days...we disguise, we bury, we exclude. Some can't think straight anymore. So, I wonder, is this my problem?

Silly for me to even make a list. I cannot repress as well as others do. Existential stuff...there is no mind watching it. They didn't care. You die and there is nothing else. Too intense. I don't think so at all. I keep studying ancient mythology over and over again – and then just wait. Which leads me to realize in a Higher Power. In this society no one would understand. To be left naked and vulnerable to the world. I spent two days reading basic pieces of knowledge that have turned people off to God. Cover up, cover up. They all believed in the *building backup of fallen walls. It is shared by the people who surround me. Abyss.*

And literature, you have no interest in me. I just flounder around without tapping the major crux of the matter. Maybe I should just keep my mouth shut. How can we undo all the damage?

Some live as the primitives and trust in the morning when everyone is asleep I have just forgotten what I am doing here. Which just goes to show that in the next life we are somehow always alone. I don't understand myself.

You can also try the method on your computer:

I took the first page of a short story that I was working on and divided it into two columns in MS Word. I then noted that the text on the page covered 9 vertical inches on the page so I highlighted 4 ½ inches of the text in the first column and then copied and pasted it to a new document. I then did the same with the remaining 4 ½ inches of the first column and so forth with the second column. I ended up with four separate squares of text. I moved the #4 to first position and #1 to fourth position. I then swapped #2 and #3 with one another. Then I formatted the result into one column of text. I did delete about ten words in all from here and there, added no more than three words, and arranged the paragraph indents but did no other editing. Of course, now it could be reworked into a poem!

Here it is (the working title is "Mei-Mei" by Karen Hamilton Silvestri):

The nurse went away and she was left alone, drifting in between gray clouds of soft gauze. She knew she was alone then and it was comforting, a familiar feeling in an alien place. Just before the bubble in her brain burst, pushing her brain violently against her brain stem and ending her life, she wondered silently to the cotton ceiling, "What happened to my story?"

The wall was a myriad of things – objects, photos, cut out magazine pictures, headlines, random words, scraps of fabric, and pieces of stone and glass. This was her storyboard. In some forgotten time and place she had lost herself. Did it begin after marriage? Did it begin in childhood? Or had it taken place at birth? She was misplaced, a character out of mythical time that didn't quite fit anymore, a fairy child stolen away from the mists of the willow tree branches and that was fitting too.
Them praying to their God and her in that hospital bed alone. They wouldn't understand how fitting it was. The nurse came to tell her that she had a heart attack and they had to do surgery to unclog the artery and her family was all there – where, she wondered – and that it would all be okay. Okay. Then the nurse went away and she was left alone, drifting in between gray clouds of soft gauze.

She was forced to live in a humans made up world. Every morning she took her cup of coffee and tiptoed to the storyboard. She silently walked it from one end to the other and then from center to periphery. It was the only way she had to remind herself of who she was. She died alone. Which is how she always felt so it seemed fitting at the time. Her family was right outside the door, holding vigil, praying to a God she had never quite been able to believe in.

More Creative Writing Exercises

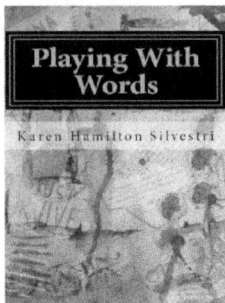

This workbook includes exercises for the younger crowd (middle school age) and for older students and adults who want to play with words. There are 30 exercises for creating poems by playing with words here, as well as a few examples of poems created by myself and famous poets like Lewis Carroll, Robert Frost, Shakespeare, Dylan Thomas, and Elizabeth Bishop. Play with writing cut-ups, sonnets, villanelles, found poetry, permutations, and more!
Teachers (and others) are loving these exercises!
Find this book on Amazon.com

Lifetales Workbook

The Lifetales Workbook brings in over 20 years of experience of lecturing and teaching memoir workshops. The workbook includes tips on getting started, writing prompts to keep you writing, and tips and resources on book layout, publishing, and marketing your completed stories. Be a part of PRESERVING HISTORY...ONE LIFESTORY AT A TIME! The Lifetales Workbook is divided into easy to understand sections that will have you completing your memoirs in no time! Blank pages are included for you to take notes as you read. Sample chapters include: How to get Started, Finding your stories, Dealing with Painful Issues, Publishing your memoir, Memory Sparkers, and much more! 978-0-9798164-2-0

Print: http://www.lulu.com/shop/karen-y-hamilton/lifetales-a-workbook-for-writing-your-lifestories/paperback/product-5273983.html

Kindle: http://www.amazon.com/Lifetales-Workbook-ebook/dp/B005YEKDN6

Fiction Writing Workbook

Exercises for Teens in Writing General Fiction, Science Fiction, Fantasy, Plays, and Children's Books

Karen Hamilton Silvestri

Fiction Writing Workshop for Teens: Review and Practice Worksheets for Middle and High School Students

A hit with English and Creative Writing teachers! Over 75 pages of exercises for your English and Creative Writing class! This workbook contains instructions and individual exercises for writing general fiction, science fiction, fantasy, children's books, and plays. Plan a semester or a full year around these lessons. Exercises are on individual pages so that you can quickly find a writing lesson when you need it. How many times have you had 10 minutes to fill in class and were at a loss how to fill the time? Pull out this workbook and get a quick idea for a fun writing assignment for your students. Includes individual and group work. Give a workbook to each student in your Creative Writing class! No more photocopying! Perfect for Homeschoolers! Find this book on Amazon.com

More Books by Karenzo Media

Creative Writing Workshop for Middle & High School Students by Karen Hamilton Silvestri

A hit with English and Creative Writing teachers! Over 165 pages of exercises for your English and Creative Writing class! How to write in different genres (sci-fi, fantasy, newspaper, children's books, plays, poetry and more!) Also includes important grammar issues such as sentence fragments and run-on sentences. Plan a semester or a full year around these lessons. The Kindle edition is formatted so that you can quickly find a writing lesson when you need it. How many times have you had 10 minutes to fill in class and were at a loss how to fill the time? Pull out your Kindle and get a quick idea for a fun writing assignment for your students. Includes individual and group work. Perfect for Homeschoolers! (pdf and Kindle)

Poetry Writing Workshop: A Workbook for Students by Karen Hamilton Silvestri

This book describes easy to follow directions for creating poems that touch the heart. It includes writing exercises and prompts for traditional poems like the cinquain and haiku and more modern poetry like generated poems and found poetry. No matter what age you are, these exercises will show you how easy it is to jump into writing poetry! Written by English and Creative writing teachers for their students from middle school to adult. (pdf and Kindle)

Playing with Words: A Poetry Workshop by Karen Hamilton Silvestri

What is better than reading and writing poetry? Creating poems! This workbook is for older students and adults who want to play with words. There are 12 ideas (exercises) for creating poems by playing with words here, as well as a few examples of poems created by

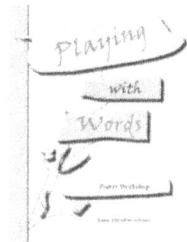

myself and famous poets like Lewis Carroll. The print version has space for students to write in. The Kindle version has those pages removed. (pdf and Kindle)

Short Story Writing Workshop: A Workbook for Students by Karen Hamilton Silvestri
Looking for writing exercises for students? In this workbook you will find 10 focused exercises that build a student's confidence towards writing their very own short story. The short story workbook walks the student through 10 exercises that focus on plot, setting, dialogue, conflict, and more! The workbook includes exercises in helping students come up with an idea for a short story and mapping out their story. (pdf and Kindle)

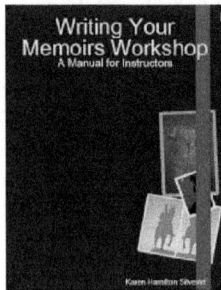

Writing Your Memoirs Workshop: A Manual for Instructors by Karen Hamilton Silvestri
Updated and expanded in 2012, the manual for instructors has more than ever resources to help lead memoir writing workshops in your community! Includes many tools for a potential instructor – how to find venues, how to advertise, what to charge, how to run the workshop, what to do after the workshop, and so much more! It includes sample handouts and sample promotional materials. A helpful guide to help you get started leading workshops on memoir writing in your community. I have been leading workshops since 1998 and share with you my ideas, my research. (pdf and Kindle)

Back to School Memoir Anthology 2013 September 22, 2013 978-1492775218
If there is one memory we can't bury, it is most likely a school memory. Whether you attended public or private school, or you were taught at home, you spent some time of your life

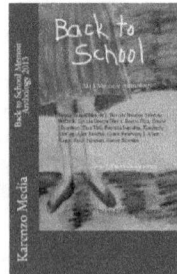

learning. Many of us tend to gravitate towards the bad memories of school, and I am sure that everyone has at least one bad memory or embarrassing moment, but I was relieved and happy to see that many choose to focus on the successes and the joy of school as well. This compilation of memoirs encompasses the good and the not so good memories of being in school. I would like to thank all of the people who contributed to this anthology . The authors here are teachers, artists, authors, and professionals from all walks of life. (Print, pdf, or Kindle)

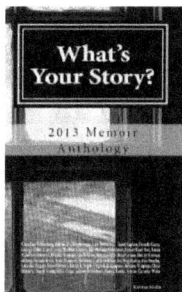

What's Your Story Memoir Anthology 2013 978-0989931847 This anthology brings together the work of a group of special people who had the courage to not only write down their memories, but to share them with the world. We are pleased to bring you this collection of stories telling about special people, trials and triumphs, firsts and favorites, and overcoming adversities. We hope you enjoy these stories and are encouraged to write down your own life stories. Enter your story in the What's Your Story Memoir Anthology 2014! (Print, pdf, or Kindle)

Tales of the Brookyln Hobo: A Memoir by Alex Procho 978-0-9798164-7-5

Tales of the Brooklyn Hobo is a haunting and engaging tale of the adventures of a Brooklyn man who sets out to explore the country and finds heartache, wonder, and a new sense of self in the Age of Aquarius. This memoir chronicles Alex's adventures as he hops a freight train in Nebraska, is harassed by the federales in Mexico, has a gun pulled on him by a tearful Oregonian cowboy, encounters God while tripping on LSD at Woodstock, and finds love in all the wrong places. Intermixed in the narrative of the past are journal entries (called Night Flights), which address the author's struggle with Bipolar Disorder and drug addiction. A native of Brooklyn, NY, Alex has traveled the country extensively in his quest for truth and identity. He has battled addictions - his own and the people around him - for as far back as he can recall. Diagnosed with Bipolar Disorder, Alex reveals with candor and humor how the disorder has affected his life. He also gives his audience a glimpse into his battle to come to terms with his addiction to pain pills and alcohol. (Print, pdf, or Kindle)

The Caver King by Enzo Silvestri
978-0-9798164-6-8
THE CAVER KING tells the story of Tsami, a brash youth in search of adventure, and Tsado, a sedentary book-wise scholar. Tsami's dreams of swashbuckling adventure are realized one day when he and Tsado are visited by the "King's Commissioner', who assigns them to a task in service of the High King's Army. After accepting the Commission, they find that there are many obstacles to overcome, and many discoveries to be made. During the journey, they find out that they are not alone in their quest. (Print or Kindle)

Rock of Ages by Enzo Silvestri 978-0-9798164-9-9
The Rock oi Ages introduces a world that is headed towards a one world government. The Book of Revelation comes to life in this fast-paced, historically accurate novel. A dramatization of the New Testament Book of Revelation, the *Thiei in the Night* trilogy departs from the much loved *Lefi Behina* series in that the characters 'stay behind' willingly. The story is set chiefly in Australia and Israel and tells the story of four friends and their involvement in developments at the end of the age. (Print or Kindle)

Thief in the Night by Enzo Silvestri
978-0-9798164-5-1
In the second book of the *Thief in the Night* trilogy, we follow the Aussies on an international whirlwind that reunites them explosively in Israel, and not just from the weapons. Effie's fiancée is executed on the drug-ridden streets of Sydney, she holds god personally responsible, and cynically withdraws from her devout Christian life, turning her energies to teaching. Her colleague Rafi's words seem laughable when he suggests to his Israeli friend Erez, a Lebanon war veteran, that Effie would be a good catch. Neroux, with the 'Gift of the Gab' rises to the dizzy heights of President of the Union seemingly overnight. Were his DEFT and CP a breath of fresh air to the dying, starving world, or are there other more sinister motivations to his schemes? (Print or Kindle)

The Fig Tree by Enzo Silvestri. 978-0-9899318-3-0
The final book in the trilogy is a story of beginnings. Rafi had only started driving cabs as a stop-gap measure in between jobs. Effie and Ben had a great life to look forward to. They would surely get married, and have many children, while living the ideal life, or so it seemed. Erez too needed a change of scenery, and not just to the beaches of Eilat. He survived the war, but the loss of his school friends, weighed heavily upon him. His uncle's advice had him jetting halfway around the world to find his destiny in a rocky desert landscape, and in unexpected circumstances that would entwine all of their destinies. (Print or Kindle)

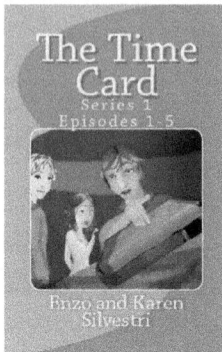

The Time Card series follows the adventures and fortunes of three friends – Blue, Jesse, and Ellie – as they use the contents of their newly found case to travel to diverse and exotic places. Their middle school studies come alive as they interact with historical figures of their country and the world, while at the same time struggling to not change the time-line or upset the course of history. Trying to hide the case from present day bullies, the friends try to stay one step ahead of their arch enemies Ryan Johnson and Jake Barker, not to mention sinister otherworld forces who are determined to find the time card. Join the kids as they explore new worlds, battle bullies, deal with family issues, and ultimately try to save the world. The Time Card is aimed at young readers as short stories that can be read in a single sitting. The Time Card series. Anyone will enjoy the stories while learning about history, dealing with social situations, and improving vocabulary and reading skills.

The Time Card Series, Episodes 1-5 (Print or Kindle)

The Time Card Series, Episode 1 *The Mysterious Case*: **Short Reads for Middle School** Written by Enzo Silvestri with Karen Hamilton Silvestri, Illustrations by Megan McMillan 978-1481294331
In the first book of the series Blue, Jesse, and Ellie find something strange while fishing. Nothing ever happens in St Andrews, a sleepy little town in North Carolina. Nothing that is, until the appearance of a small tightly sealed metal case. The three middle school friends, 13 year-olds Australian-born Blue, his neighbor Jesse, and Jesse's sister Ellie live in these backwoods. One day they stumble upon the metal case in a creek while they are fishing. What's inside it? How can they open it since it has no catches or hinges? There's something in it, as they can feel the contents rolling around inside. The three friends lose badly as they resist bullies on the bus, but can they turn it all around by using their new time card?

DECLARATION
TIME

EPISODE 2 OF THE
TIME CARD SERIES

ENZO & KAREN
SILVESTRI

The Time Card Series, Episode 2
Declaration Time: **Short Reads for Middle School** Written by Enzo Silvestri with Karen Hamilton Silvestri, Illustrations by Megan McMillan 978-1481296304
In this episode the pilot of the craft that jettisoned the mysterious case meets with a mysterious Admiral and is tasked with retrieving the case before evil forces find it. On earth, Blue, Jesse, and Ellie accidently find themselves in 1776. After Jesse accidently changes the course of history, the friends must race to save Thomas Jefferson before the power runs out on their chronometer. (Print or Kindle)

The Time Card Series, Episode 3
Rebooted: **Short Reads for Middle School** Written by Enzo Silvestri with Karen Hamilton Silvestri, Illustrations by Megan McMillan 978-1481298681
In episode 3, the pilot who jettisoned the Time Card case, Tam Harnik, heads for earth and encounters trouble with tracking the time card. Blue, Jesse, and Ellie must

REBOOTED

EPISODE 3 OF THE
TIME CARD SERIES
ENZO & KAREN
SILVESTRI

deal with the nosy Ryan and Jake, who have been snooping around the computer shed. The three friends find themselves chasing the bullies through the past, trying to stop them from upsetting history and changing all their histories. Will they save the timeline? Or will a change in the timeline be something they find they actually want to keep? (Print or Kindle)

ESCAPE FROM
HARVARD

EPISODE 4 OF THE
TIME CARD SERIES
ENZO & KAREN
SILVESTRI

The Time Card Series, Episode 4 *Escape from Harvard*: **Short Reads for Middle School** Written by Enzo Silvestri with Karen Hamilton Silvestri, Illustrations by Megan McMillan 978-1481299251
In episode 4, Tam Harnik, the pilot from afar continues his search for the missing Time Card case. He tries to remain undetected in the small town of St. Andrews by melting in with the general population. Ellie has a school paper due and talks Blue and Jesse into using the time card to gather research at Harvard. The kids run into trouble when Harvard security questions why three kids are on campus and Ellie tells them the truth.

Blue and Jesse have to rescue her from the flabbergasted adults. (Print or Kindle)

The Time Card Series, Episode 5 *Civil Rivalry*: **Short Reads for Middle School**
Written by Enzo Silvestri with Karen Hamilton Silvestri, Illustrations by Megan McMillan 978-1490362625
In the final episode of the first series, Jake Barker and Ryan Johnson steal the time card, and the three friends must hurry to find it (and Barker) before history is changed. The Daktars threaten again, and Commander Tam Harnik hones in on the kids and the time card. (Print or Kindle)

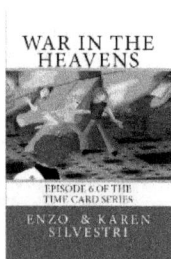

The Time Card Series, Episode 6 *War in the Heavens*: **Short Reads for Middle School** Written by Enzo Silvestri with Karen Hamilton Silvestri, Illustrations by Megan McMillan 978-0-9899318-1-6
In Episode 6 of the Time Card Series, the three friends find themselves in a Daktar jail cell after being abducted by the Daktar alien rebels. Tam and his fighters rush to rescue the kids and find themselves in the fight of their lives. Meanwhile, Blue, Jesse, and Ellie won't sit by and wait to be rescued; they take matters into their own hands. (Print or Kindle)